To Ka[illegible] my Beloved Friend - Always - TMS Steele

THE MIND OF STEELE

Jan 22. 2023

DISCOVER THE MIND OF STEELE

THE INVINCIBLE JOURNEY OF 7 DECADES TO BECOMING AGELESS, FEARLESS, AND DIVINELY CONNECTED.

TRISH STEELE

The Gail Grace Nordskog Collection

Discover the Mind of Steele: The Invincible Journey of 7 Decades to Becoming Ageless, Fearless, and Divinely Connected.

by Trish Steele

ISBN: 978-1-80128-335-9

Cover Photographer: William Kidston

Editing Consultant: Benediction.biz

Dedication

To my grandmother: Carmen Saad, who was the beam of light in my life. She saw something in me at a very young age. "*You are special.*" She would say these three words of encouragement to me all the time. These three words were like a banner of hope that stayed with me all these years!

To my daughters: Shawna Jean Sherburne and Michelle Haddad Steele, who are strong, patient, and full of compassion for others. My hope is that you both will take the legacy that I have built to the next level, saving lives as the world goes through its changes. Thank you for the years of patience and understanding toward me while your mom was so busy saving lives and helping others.

To the readers: This book is dedicated to you to inspire you to open yourself up to something greater than you've ever experienced. To fulfill the true calling in your life. "*You are special*" to me for selecting this book. I am excited for a new journey that you are about to experience and be divinely connected to.

It is my privilege and honor to know Trish Steele. She has ministered to me with great wisdom and compassion for thirty-five years in my acting career and my personal success. I owe her a huge thanks for connecting me with the president of CBS Studios, which allowed me to teach my non-denominational sermons there at the studio for the first six years of my worldwide ministry.

—Lee Benton

Trish gave me strength to speak my truth and opened the door to many avenues that helped me heal from past pain and mistreatment. She is one of the kindest, most loving, and supportive people I've ever met, and she is nothing short of an angel on this earth.

—Sophie Turner

Trish's passion for helping women spurred me into my destiny with more clarity and resilience. In addition, her loving, compassionate mentorship encouraged me during stormy times in my life, and she is one of my most treasured friends.

—Kathleen O'Donnell Dew

Trish was consultant for my non-profit charity and coached me with every business I was doing. Her guidance, expertise, and highly positive, motivating attitude were important factors in my success!

—Agnes-Nicole Winter

After reaching success in my traditional business and becoming a mother for the first time, I realized that I was living in unhealed trauma. Trish's anointed mindset, coaching, and incredible wisdom helped me in acknowledging the childhood secret that was blocking me from living a life of purpose and healing.

—Janet Cano

Trish Steele is a fabulous woman who has been mentoring me since the first time my organization, "Mi Amor Gala," did an event to raise funds for Safe Passage. She has become an ongoing consultant and a great motivator in encouraging me to continue to expand my message of kindness and inspiration to women around the world.

—Luisa Diaz Brown

CONTENTS

Foreword

Since being given the honor of writing the foreword to Trish Steele's incredible story of her life's journey, I have been wrestling with how best to approach the task. I put together several different drafts, trying to write as persuasively as I could, because I so fervently want for you, the reader, to realize what a treasure you hold in your hands. I wish for you to know that this book can change your life, for the Glory of God!

I believe God has shown me the best way to make my case. That is, to share what I know about Trish from our thirty-year friendship and why I believe those who read her story will be inspired, transformed, and set free from lies.

These are the attributes I see in this godly woman, Trish Steele:

Physically, she is beautiful and cares for her body as a temple of God.

As for her character, I have always found her to be compassionate, kind, gracious, joyful, honest, trustworthy, inspiring, loving, forgiving, adventurous, strong, bold, and courageous.

Spiritually, Trish has not only been shaped into a godly woman through hardship and faith, but she has undergone the discipline of becoming an ordained Christian pastor, and she is a gifted teacher. Her story and her example are an inspiration.

For all these reasons, I am blessed and honored to include this autobiography of my dear friend Trish Steele in my *Gail Grace Nordskog Collection*, which is a selection of writings I've chosen to offer as particularly empowering and inspiring to women in our unique giftings and life challenges.

As you get to know Trish the way I do, you will begin to realize you too are a chosen child of the Most High God, called by Him to live victoriously over ALL the lies you may have been believing about yourself. Trish's trials and victories will encourage you to be an overcomer and live your fullest life!

Enjoy this life-changing journey!

Gail Grace Nordskog

Author, *Hearts of Purpose*, Volume 1: The Call

Co-Publisher, Nordskog Publishing, Inc

Introduction

On January 9, 2020, I attended a vision-board class in Santa Monica. There were twenty attendees participating in this class. As the instructor gave us inspiration to create a vision board, my mind focused on my life vision. I allowed my spirit to take over this process and lead me to the things that I was to accomplish. I began with a list of personal goals for myself and then the goals for my non-profit businesses.

Ideas began to flow freely and rapidly as I searched through many magazines for images to fit onto my vision board. At completion, my board showed a healthy, peaceful, and enjoyable lifestyle, one of leisure and freedom. It showed a new neighborhood and a place called home. It's been said, "Write the vision down so that you may run with it," and that is exactly what I did with the vision board. I was so excited to be the first one to finish my board and to share it with others in the class.

My vision began to manifest the following month, while looking for a new home to move to. I wanted to move somewhere peaceful so I could retire. On March 27, 2020, the COVID pandemic hit California and the entire U.S. So many were in fear of getting sick and possibly dying from COVID 19. But for me, it brought an urgency to leave Los Angeles. And my family and I did so on July 1, moving to Westlake Village, a beautiful community.

It was a miracle to find a home during this time, with a landlord that would trust us to pay the high rental fees. During this time, many people lost their jobs, their health, their financial support, and their sanity.

The move to Westlake Village was simultaneous with my realization of the monumental change the world was undergoing— change at a level I'd never experienced. It caused a revolution in my mindset, which in turn caused shifting priorities and goals in my life.

I did not realize this was the manifestation of my vision board. From my retirement mindset, I began to hear the Spirit of God speaking to me about a new purpose, even while the world was quaking in heartbreaking ways. These are the exact words that God spoke to my heart:

1. I want you to write your life story, a journey of seventy years.
2. This book will cover seven decades; each chapter will represent one decade and will include the history of that time in your life.
3. There is redemption in each chapter, and it will bring hope to many.
4. Your legacy will live forever, and many will embrace it.

5. I will bring the right connections to you to bring this all about.

I felt this was impossible to accomplish because of the cost of thousands of dollars and hundreds of hours. "I moved away from the busy city to retire and take life easy. I am content with my life and not interested in another project or adventure," I responded to God.

I took another look at my vision board after seven months and realized that there were more steps I needed to take to complete my vision. Life is full of surprises and can be very exciting if we follow the guidance of the One who created life to begin with.

So, I accepted God's assignment, and this is the result. To you readers this book is written, to challenge you not to give up on your purpose in life, but to embrace what is good so you may live a life of happiness. "It's not how you begin your journey, but how you finish your journey." Join me in discovering the Mind of Steele to gain insight into an ageless, fearless, and divinely connected lifestyle.

Trish surrounds herself with people that are like minded: compassionate, kind, gracious, joyful, honest, trustworthy, inspiring, loving, strong, forgiving, courageous, and adventurous. She's a Dancing Queen!

Chapter 1

The '50s: I Was Not Planned For This World

The 1950s were called the "Happy Days" for multiple reasons. First, we had finished a huge war, and our economy was booming. As a result, during the 1950s many social booms took place. It was a starry night in September, and a young girl aged fifteen was all set to have a good time at the Catholic church in Los Angeles, where a monthly dance was taking place. A young man aged twenty-two was also getting ready to attend the same dance that night. They knew not of each other's existence or what the future held for them.

This young girl was named Lorraine, and her appearance was much more appealing than her name. The beauty she had is still unmatched—beautiful, long, wavy hair falling down her back and those sparkling eyes. There was magic in her eyes. To see her was to fall in love with her. Men craved the graceful curves of her beautiful body. She exuded grace and beauty that resembled the actress Jane Russell.

This beautiful young girl, who was part Lebanese, American Indian, and Spanish, reached the Catholic church of her neighborhood with two girlfriends. The aforementioned young man, half English and half Mexican, Harry Aurelio Blanco, was also there. As the night took off, the young man looked at this young girl and instantly fell for her beautiful eyes, charming personality, and the aura that surrounded her.

At that very moment, Harry knew he wanted to spend the rest of his life with this Lorraine, so they began to date. They would spend their days together learning about each other and falling deeply in love. The love and romance between them increased to the point that the world outside became secondary.

One day they decided to meet at Lorraine's house, since her parents were not home. At first, they were all chill, chatting with each other, but over time things got steamy between them. They were suddenly naked, having passionate sex. It was the very first time for Lorraine, and the love of her life took her virginity.

A while later, Lorraine was expecting her first child with the man she loved with all her heart. And that unplanned child that was about to enter the baby-boom generation was me. This was the generation considered the most hardworking, productive, and upwardly mobile in the world. The baby boomers are those 76 million born after the Second World War. They rejected and redefined traditional values. They are also the wealthiest, most active, and possessing the highest disposable income for food, apparel, and retirement programs. I was about to be born to a beautiful couple who loved each other to the moon and back. Both were fun loving and outgoing people who came from big families that embraced responsibility. My father was also passionate and hardworking. My parents would do anything for each other and their families to make them happy.

Knowing that I was about to come into this world, they decided to marry.

Now it was time to find a name for me, while taking their first trip to the hospital—not knowing if I would be a boy or a girl. Today, thanks to ultrasound equipment that scans your belly for the baby's gender, naming a child and preparation of the baby room are so much easier. Lorraine and Harry announced the arrival of a healthy baby girl named Patricia Jean Blanco.

Do you ever wonder what made your parents pick out your name? I sure did, because I was not excited about my name—especially my nickname, Patty. Other kids in school used to call me "Patty-Cake." A silly but popular short song of the era goes like this:

Pat-a-cake, pat-a-cake baker's man. Bake me a cake as fast as you can. Pat it and prick it and mark it with "B." Put it in the oven for baby and me.

As I got older, I researched my name to find out what it meant. Patricia, meaning the "noble one," was the second most common female name in the United States according to the 1990 U.S. census. My name was to be tested in the journey that lay before me. Remember to name your children with positive meaning, for it is a big part of their DNA and life calling. Back to my family. My father worked day and night as a carpenter to provide the best for his family. With a child coming into this world, his responsibilities were about to double. Even so, my dad managed to buy a house in Norwalk, California, just two years after marrying my mom.

Harry was an amazing father. He was always the husband and father who wanted the best for his family. He wanted us to have the best education, clothing, and environment to live in. So, I would always say that I was a daddy's girl! My mother, on the other hand, was busy having babies and gave birth to another daughter and a son after me. My sister was named Debby Ann Blanco, and my brother, Harry Aurelio Blanco III, but he got the nickname "Butch."

My siblings had completely different personalities from mine. I was always responsible and active, while they were the naughty ones, and my mother had a tough time raising them, especially in her later years. As Daddy's Girl, I considered Dad to be the best thing about my life—not that I didn't love Mom, but she was too domestic, and Dad was the fun one. I must say that I *was* there to help her raise my siblings, as I was the oldest.

Reflecting on childhood, I would say that mine was great, as I had a perfect time growing up. I would ride my bicycle on the streets all alone without fear and spend my whole day playing with the neighborhood kids in their homes.

Well, that was a time today's generation could never relate to. They can't understand the delight of playing games like hide and seek, children's games, and the simpler toys. Instead of computer games, we had footballs, hula hoops, skipping ropes, and cards. Every mother had a sewing machine to teach her daughters sewing, and homemaking classes were what you looked forward to in middle school.

Today's world is much different than the one in which I grew up. Technology has taken over the minds of young kids and consumes all their time. I remember how we gathered in the neighborhood park at five in the evening and played until sunset. Ours was a close-knit community, where my parents were friends with my friends' parents, and we all hung out together. Life was simple back then.

But one sad day, the tables turned immensely for all of us. Life no longer remained so happy and simple.

It started when my father planned a trip to a famous local lake on 4th-of-July weekend near the mountains with a few Boy Scouts and our family. He took me, my mother, and my sister along. Since my brother was only two and a half years old, my parents left him at my grandma's house. When we reached the lake, we all were so happy. We were having a perfect time when the most tragic event of my life happened that evening.

My father was out on the water with a few of his close friends, playing tug-of-war in the canoes, when suddenly my father's canoe tipped over. He and his friends had been tipsy from drinking beer all night. Unaware of what had happened to my dad, they were laughing at the fact that they lost at tug-of-war. He was a good swimmer and tried to swim to shore, but the night had grown dark, and he couldn't see which direction to go.

After struggling for ten minutes, he became entangled in the lake's seaweed. It must have been the most terrifying moment of his life. His friends could not hear that Harry was struggling for his life. Crying for help at the top his lungs did not save him. Only God knows why these events occur in our lives.

Harry's three friends made it back to shore safely and noticed that Harry had not made it back. The men yelled out, "Harry!" repeatedly. No response. They then went to the ranger to report a missing person, but the ranger said that he would have to wait till dawn to search for him.

The rescue teams looked for Dad's body in the lake, and after a couple of hours, they found it. My mother was asked to identify the body, which she did immediately and then fainted. At the age of twenty-one, she had lost her loving husband and the love of her life. My dad was only twenty-seven years old, and he was gone. For Mom, it was the end of the world. My mother suffered a stroke that day. She had lost the biggest support of her life. She was left all alone with three little children to take care of.

I was awakened by the noise of people mourning outside near the lake. Looking out the cabin window, I saw my mother and my father's friends looking down at a body on the ground. "What's going on?" I asked. My aunt Gloria tried to protect me, "Someone is hurt, and you must stay inside." The body was my father's; he had drowned and never made it back to shore.

It was a moment of shock for all of us. We were not able to process the unthinkable. I was in tears. I could not understand what happened to my father. He was right here with me a little while ago, camping around the fire and roasting marshmallows, and now he was not here with me. Everyone was crying and mourning for my father. I had never thought of my life without him. And I was still hopeful that he would come out of the lake like a hero with his arms wide open. He would run to us with his beautiful smile and passionate heart and would hug us tightly. But many hours passed, and he did not come.

Although I was only five years old, I remember everything very clearly that day of July 4th, 1957. I remember what my mother went through after my father's death. Though she recovered physically, she was still in pain emotionally—the pain of living without the love of her life. Whenever I saw her like that, tears would roll down my cheeks. I never thought I'd see her so broken.

During that time of great emotional turmoil, she decided to leave our Norwalk house and move us to Los Angeles, closer to my grandmother, as my father's memories haunted her in that Norwalk home. She felt depressed in that house. So, she rented it out and moved to Los Angeles. There, we got an apartment near my grandma so she could take care of my mother and us three young kids.

My mother's condition impacted me, making me feel hopeless. I became quiet all day, lost in my own thoughts. I grieved over the loss of my dad all summer long. One thing about kids is that they don't understand loss at all. It's a huge unanswered question: Why? So that's what I asked God every day: "Why did you take my daddy away from me?"

School began, and my first-grade teacher realized that something was wrong with me. I was not paying attention or comprehending what was being taught in school. I don't think even I realized at first what was happening with me. My mother was called to the school and told about my behavior, and the teacher recommended she take me for a physical checkup.

My mother took me to a hearing specialist. After a complete checkup, he asked my mother whether I'd had any high fevers in the past. My mother recalled an incident during my childhood at age five, when I had a high fever of 105 degrees Fahrenheit, and both my parents had taken me to the hospital.

In those days, rheumatic fever was a life-threatening disease, and some people ended up with significant health issues. But the hospital doctor at that time said that the fever was going down and there was nothing much to be worried about.

Upon hearing of this incident, the hearing specialist said that high fever had damaged the nodes behind my ears, and I had lost 70 percent of my hearing ability. This hearing specialist recommended hearing aids for me, and he also suggested my mother get me admitted to a school for "deaf and dumb people." In the 1950s, schools for the hearing impaired were labeled as "deaf-and-dumb schools." My mom looked for some time for the best such school in Los Angeles and finally got me enrolled in one called Mary E. Bennett School.

Being placed in that school was the worst experience of my life. I was placed right in front of the teacher at a desk, with no one next to me, to learn a new technique called "lip reading." I asked myself, What?? I was faced with another adversity in my life, making me feel lonely and punished by God.

And bullying is nothing new. I was bullied even at this school for not knowing sign language. The other students would all communicate with each other through sign language, and it looked to me like a bunch of angry kids cursing each other in hand gestures that flew around like mad. I was placed at this school to learn the new lip-reading technique. I found this way of communication interesting. It was a fun thing to read someone's lips and know what they were trying to communicate. My strong interest helped me learn this technique before all the others, and I was therefore one of the first to lip-read successfully. I guess I was the successful guinea pig!

However, in the crowd of all those bullies, one student was cooperative with me. She would communicate with me by reading my lips to show that she cared and wanted to be my friend. Still, I would come home every day, crying to my grandma, asking, "Why me?" Why had God been so unkind to me? First, He took my daddy away from me, then He took my hearing away, and now I was being bullied by kids who were just like me. But, as Grandma would always say, "Patty, things will be okay. God is testing you because you are special." These three words, "*You are special*," were enough to make me feel good. I would instantly feel motivated to fight my battle against the world's tragedies and personal traumas.

My grandmother was a hardcore Catholic. She would go to church nearly every day. She was a firm believer, which is why I feel that she had so much courage, especially to stay brave after my uncle's death (her only son), who was just seventeen years old when he passed away from a car accident. I cannot explain how she remained so composed and robust. Her reaction to her son's death was the complete opposite of my mother's when my father died. My grandmother was a woman who always had her spirits high and was always thankful to God. The way she practiced gratitude was always exemplary for me. I learned so much from her.

I would frequently go to the Catholic church near my house to light a candle and think about all the bad things that had happened to me. One day, I was sitting all alone in the church, but this time, I was not complaining to God. Instead, I thanked Him for giving me all the lovely people in my life, like my grandma, my mother, and my siblings. I had so much to be thankful for. This was the turning point for me, as I began to live life again. My mother was twenty-six by then, and she wanted to do something with her life. There was a famous bar in Long Beach called Captain Paul, where she wanted to work. This bar was a stop for all the sailors and the tourists who would visit Long Beach. Since my mother was lovely, she got a job there as a waitress.

In the meantime, my siblings, Butch, Debby, and I, lived with my grandma and my aunt Loretta, who suffered from mental illness due to rheumatic fever at the age of nine. She reminded me of that character from the horror movie called *Carrie*. You never knew when she was going to go off on you with rage and violence. These terrifying episodes of her seizures would happen once a month, and we had to run for our lives, either hiding under the beds or escaping outside up in the hills. Grandma was the only one that could stop her from badly harming us.

After a while, I became quite skillful at quickly escaping Aunt Loretta's episodes. Today, my heart goes out to so many children born with mental-health issues, including autism. I have seen hundreds of children being born with autism these past twenty years; we really need to find a cure for it. At the Mary E. Bennett School, I remember the holiday called May Day. In medieval and modern Europe, the May Day holiday (May 1) was the celebration of the return of spring. The observance probably originated in ancient agricultural rituals, as the Greeks and Romans held such festivals. They decorated poles at school, and we would dance around those poles dressed up in white blouses and festive gathered skirts. I felt so pretty and proud because my grandmother helped me with a handmade gathered skirt by showing me how to use her sewing machine. I received many compliments that day. It was the first time in a long time that I wore a huge smile, and I felt popular and accepted again.

All the people attending this special day who watched me dance were amazed. I was so happy, as dancing was my therapy. I felt like I was in some other world. Dancing was my escape from my childhood trauma. It was the only thing that would help me come out of my shell. Aunt Judy took me to the dance hall a few times, and I grew to love it! It was the only way for me to express acceptance and confidence, and I was great at it! Not only was it a joy for me, but I had enough natural talent to eventually compete in dancing competitions.

Also, I would watch TV shows like *I Love Lucy* and *Leave it to Beaver*, which made me laugh so much. Laughter is like good medicine for your soul, and as they say, we need a scoop a day. My favorite show to watch was *American Bandstand*, with the top recording artists of the '50s, like Jerry Lee Lewis, Rickey Nelson, Paul Anka, Connie Francis, and others who got all the teens dancing. Watching this show got me dancing in my own living room and having the time of my life. My favorite dance was the "Stroll," a line-up format that was so cool. Each couple would stroll in their cool movement down the aisle. We need to escape our problems through positive activities that are good for our body, soul, and spirit. Music and dancing gave me hope and allowed me to dream bigger!

By now, my mother had earned a good amount of money from her job at the bar, and she had also decided to sell our Norwalk house. She took all three of us, my siblings and me, to Long Beach with her. What an exciting move to a city that had a beach a few miles away and the Pike Amusement Park.

My mother had a nice convertible car, and one day she took a drive down Ocean Boulevard with the top down, when two young gentlemen dressed as sailors came in front of our car. They asked my mother for a ride, and guess what? One of those sailors was about to become my stepfather.

Discover Patty's Mindset

AS A YOUNG GIRL, PATTY SETS HER MIND FOR ANSWERS INSTEAD OF BEING HOPELESS. THE WORD OF GOD SAYS, "ASK, AND IT WILL BE GIVEN TO YOU; SEEK, AND YOU WILL FIND; KNOCK, AND IT WILL BE OPENED TO YOU." (MATTHEW 7:7)

Patricia Jean Blanco age seventeen, known as Trish Steele

Chapter 2

The '60s: Born To Be Wild?

As time passed, my mom got closer to this man who took a lift in her car. Mitch was so handsome, with blond hair, bright hazel eyes, and a height of more than six feet. This man's charm could make any woman fall for him. Along with a handsome face, he had a strong personality. He was the kind of person who was brave, confident, and yet self-aware. He had a military attitude, which made him distinct from other men.

He had such an authoritative personality that he would attract all attention toward himself. Whenever we were with mom and he was around, this respect commanded an attention that was different from what we had been raised with. The way he talked was so impressive, as he taught us the different levels of authority of a captain or sailor. But I would also say that being mean and aggressive were two prominent traits of his personality.

After dating for months, my mom married this man, and he moved in with us. We lived in a two-bedroom apartment, where my two other siblings and I were in one bedroom, while my mom and my stepdad lived in the other room. He took us out so that we would like him and bond with him. He made every effort to become close to us, but at home the discipline and structure was more like a boot camp.

Since he had this military attitude, he wanted us to behave militarily. He would scold us or give a smack on our heads if we did anything against the rules that he had set for us. There was a defined way of walking, sitting, and even speaking to him. He taught us a list of table manners. He would say that you should always finish whatever is on your plate, and once you are done, you should take your plate to the kitchen by yourself. All these rules were suffocating at times, but still, we were doing it for our mother and her happiness.

He would also prepare meals for us, since he was an excellent cook. Even my mom learned cooking from him. I remember one day, he made certain vegetables that I did not like. But I was forced to eat them. He forced me to eat the last bite on my plate. Once I was done, I started feeling sick. I went to the bathroom and threw up. I was crying and choking.

I felt that my mother was siding more with him and was distancing herself from us children. I remember sometimes they would drop all three of us at the movie theater so that they could spend time alone together, and when the movies ended, we would have to walk back home all alone. One day after coming out of the movie theater, we were walking along the sidewalk. A man sitting in his car yelled to me, "Little girl, do you know where Stanley Street is?" When I walked up close to his car, I saw he had his penis sticking out of his pants, and he was masturbating. How awful! I ran back to my sister and brother and grabbed their hands, and we ran all the way home.

It was my first experience seeing someone expose his privates to me, and it made me feel dirty. It was a trauma I carried with me for a long time. When my sister and I got home, I took my mother aside and shared what had happened. "Patty, that's what dirty old men do" was all she could say, which seemed an odd reaction to me. But only God knew how to keep me safe and keep me hoping for something better in life.

And all that hoping finally led to something good that did come into my life. My mom announced that she was pregnant and that we were going to have a new sibling added to the family. It was so exciting to have a baby sister I could nurture and play with. Her name was Cheryl Mitchell, a beautiful girl full of sweetness and smiles. But that was not the end of my mom's pregnancies; another child was on its way ten months later. This pregnancy was very serious, and it took all my mother's strength to deliver baby Cindy. She was a twelve-pound baby and looked just like my stepdad. She was not like us; we were all seven pounds when we were born. But I loved her and did all the caring a big sister would do. After having his own children, my stepdad became more amicable toward my siblings and me. He would get on the bed with us girls and make us laugh by tickling us. He became softer in his manner and character and watched TV with us, since we now had his two additional girls in the family. We were having fun and enjoying the "father-daughter bond."

But suddenly things changed—for the worse. My stepdad started touching me in the wrong places. This gave me a feeling of disgust. It was very awkward. I felt so much shame. I did not know how to deal with it. Why was this happening just as I felt comfortable bonding with him? Another "dirty man" was trying to take over my life. I had to shove the incidents into my gut and forget what was happening to me.

There is something I want to make clear to all readers: No one has the right to touch your body in an inappropriate way or abuse it violently with their hands. You are made beautifully in God's image and likeness, and God has placed in your soul the spirit of kindness, gentleness, respect, and feeling good about who you are. I found this out later in life, and my hope is that by sharing my story, I can bring clarity, love, and restoration to your soul.

We were still in Long Beach. I was learning to be very good at lip-reading, and my speech therapy was ongoing. My new school was a lot better than my previous school. Here there were some blind kids as well, who would learn from unique books made for them to "read" by touching the words with their hands.

One day, I saw someone being rude to some blind students. I saw them being bullied, so I decided to be their advocate. I stood up for their rights and tried my level best to protect them. I could not just stand there and watch other kids bully them. It was wrong! So, I would walk them to their classes to make sure no one would bully them. In school, I learned to be compassionate and grateful for my life when I could see that others had it worse.

Since I was not allowed to watch my favorite dance show, *American Bandstand* (orders from my stepdad), I decided to create my own show. Well, yes, I did. I used our garage very creatively and made a stage studio. At that time, I was only ten years old, but still, my passion and love for dance made me take this huge step. I did everything on my own and turned that garage into a comfortable stage.

That studio was my escape from all my problems. I would dance there and sing there as if I were a movie star. I applied everything I learned by watching television and remembering scenes from many shows. I would direct my sister Debby and brother Butch in the scenes of my productions. It was the beginning of my career in the television industry that would blossom in future years. If you are going through any trauma or past disappointments in life, you may want to consider escaping into something you love. It will bring healing and confidence as you move along in this journey called life!

Six months later, my stepfather got transferred to a new city, Burbank. Wow, a new adventure and a big house! I felt so happy there in a new neighborhood, and I had hope for a new group of friends. Our new house had four bedrooms, so my sister and I got a bedroom of our own to share. At that time, we bonded so well and became so close that we were inseparable. My sister was a source of joy for me.

One evening while sleeping in bed, I felt my stepfather's hands under my sheets touching me again in the private parts of my body. I froze. I wanted to pretend that I did not feel his presence next to me, and I kept my eyes closed. In my mind, all I could think was that this was wrong, and I wondered how I would face this mean stepfather.

His unwelcome night visits did not stop there but went on for months, with touching and breathing heavily and whispers that I could not understand, for I was partially deaf. It was not the end of his shameful acts but just the beginning. One day he came very close to me, grabbed my hand, and took me to the bathroom. He did his shameful deed, exposing himself like a dirty old man, and said, "If you ever tell your mother, she will leave you, and you will be left in an orphanage."

I was only eleven years old. He said that he would make everyone believe that I was a dirty girl. At that time, no resources were available to find help because everyone kept these sorts of violations as "the dirty little secret." So many people have carried around their dark, dirty, and shameful secrets for years until women like me were raised to expose the secrets and get support to heal our lives. I will be sharing more of this later.

Middle school had just begun for me in Burbank, with another challenge ahead of me, just like the past schools. I was more confident with my speech and hearing loss this time, knowing how to communicate better without feeling like a "dumb retard" girl. I met a few new friends, but little did I know they were into drugs, alcohol, and parties. These new friends would take me to their friends' homes, where drugs were being passed out. I was being influenced by the new world of drugs and alcohol at the young age of thirteen.

I still remember clearly how the drugs affected my mind. They numbed me of all my pain from life's disappointments and hurts, but they never solved my problems. Over the years, kids and teens who have been trying drugs to numb their pain have ended up in addictions that cannot be broken. Some have ended in the grave through overdoses. Drugs destroy lives, kill, and take you away from your purpose in life.

The '60s were the start of a revolution and a new movement that captured many minds with deadly drugs. It was a miracle that I eventually walked away from using drugs.

I would spend my whole day with these friends because going home was awful for me. My stepfather used to tell me that I was no longer of worth—that I was stupid and would never amount to anything. But those words from my grandmother were still ringing in my ears, "Patty, *you are special*." I was determined to fight off those awful words spoken by my stepfather. It was not easy, and I began to find different avenues to fight thoughts of him.

Times were changing in the ’60s. Teens were creating an era of freedom and fighting for social change with the hippie and Civil Rights movements. I became bold, needing to share the secrets of my molestation and dysfunctional lifestyle at home. I no longer wanted this dark secret to stay inside me. There came a moment when I decided to share it with my sister Debby. “Our stepfather has been molesting me. What should I do? I want to tell it to Mom or run away and start living on my own.” While I was sharing all these things with her, she said, “Patty, he did the same to me.” I was shocked. I could not take the fact that he was doing those dirty things to my sister too.

Now it became intolerable for me. I could no longer let it stay a secret any longer. This had to change for the protection of my sister and myself.

We both decided that we could not live this way anymore, even if we had to run away from home. We were only thirteen and twelve years old, but we were mature enough to be brave and run away. So we got up, wiped each other’s tears, and went to Mom.

We made her sit at the kitchen table. At that time, luckily, our stepdad was not at home. Our mother was speechless. As she was hearing us out, Debby and I could see that her life was caving in emotionally, and she was holding the tears and anger in her soul. In the end, she said, “Don’t worry, girls, next time he does anything to you, you should come and tell me right away." I asked my mother, "So, you won't be leaving us, Mom?" To this, she replied, "Of course not." That is what our stepdad would say to us about our mom—that she would leave us if we ever said anything to her.

She mustered enough courage to say something to my stepdad, which made him stop molesting us. But it did not prevent the abuse—spanking us with belts and verbal abuse. My mother did not tell us, but our stepdad was mean to her too. He was rude toward my mother and made her feel worthless every single day. He would go out after his day at work, seeing other women, and come home late at night. This was the beginning of my mom's plan to find a way out of the marriage.

I am so grateful that domestic violence, abuse, molestation, and sexual harassment are considered wrong and immoral today, and you can be sent to jail for them. In the '50s and '60s, there were no laws for discrimination against women and children in the home settings. Only in recent decades have advocates against such abuse created rescue shelters and services for safety. Women and teens are now going out and telling their stories on both public and private platforms. They no longer feel scared, shameful about it, or controlled and trapped by another person who is violating their bodies. Never hold on to this secret! Tell someone or call the police. We all need to be treated morally and with respect because we are special—*you are special*, and God loves you.

I was still hanging out with the same friends, and older kids who had cars would pick me up and take me to different parties. It was another eye-opener, and I knew that I needed to fit in to become part of the group. "Hollywood, here I come!" I shouted as we cruised down Hollywood Boulevard, under the influence of LSD. This drug was a white pill that the hippie movement spread in the '60s to have psychedelic encounters in the hopes of promoting the new era of peace. The drug destroyed many minds, causing people to attempt suicide without realizing they were doing it. But the reality was, Hollywood and its counterculture movement ushered in a cultural downfall and much destruction.

Many of us remember the famous actress Marilyn Monroe, who was emblematic of the era's sexual revolution. So many people wanted to be like her, only to find out that she suffered from depression from all the alcohol, drugs, sex, and manipulation of the Hollywood fame machine. That self-destructive spirit overtook her after she realized that stardom only gave her temporary happiness. The sex symbol committed suicide, and today, many other famous people have done the same. I hope you do not fall for this trap. Be yourself! Get God's purpose for your life!

Another famous person who comes to mind that shook our country was President Kennedy. I was in school, and every morning the teacher would lead us in our daily prayer. After that prayer on November 22, 1963, someone came into the classroom and announced that President Kennedy had just been shot. This news came as a shock to all of us students. People belonging to all age groups loved him, especially those that were fighting for their place in life through the Civil Rights Movement, the Cold War, and the Vietnam War. He was the youngest president and was Catholic. His extraordinary charisma and charm made him universally beloved. To this day, historians continue to rank him among the best-loved presidents in American history.

As life went on, I experienced more of Burbank, a city of leisure. It is the home of Walt Disney Studios and Warner Bros. Studio, not to mention the famous Bob's Big Boy drive-in restaurant. It was a safe town. I got my first job at a dry-cleaning outlet, checking in the clothes that middle-class people needed laundered. I was only fourteen years old; in those days small businesses hired teens to work. I felt so grown up, as the job allowed me to be self-sufficient. My favorite memories were having my mom and her girlfriends come to my work on a slow day to have me style their hair. My mom and I had a special bond after our conversation in which I divulged the actions of her husband, Mitch.

I was born with a natural talent for doing hair, makeup, and fashion. I was known to be the fashionable girl who always had her makeup and hair looking stylish at school. I began to believe in my natural abilities, in spite of my hearing loss and speech impairment. Have you ever seen the '60s hairdos? My favorite hairstyle at that time was the "Beehive." It would take me two hours to tease, curl, and pile the hair up high to perfection.

Our family went through big changes, trying to find happiness. My brother, Butch, became a rebel and was getting into trouble in school. Our stepdad, Mitch, made it difficult for my brother to live in the house because he would abuse Butch emotionally and physically. Debby, my sister, was becoming more and more like a tomboy and hated our home life and Mitch. Mitch would never abuse his own daughters; they got special privileges. I loved my little sisters, and they loved us three older siblings. They saw the tension between us all, and later, in their teen years, their dad's true colors came out to hurt them too.

Mitch got promoted again to a new location with his job. Now we are all about to make another move to a small town called La Verne. It was south of the big city, about one hour away, and this city was full of orange groves—farmland, with trees for miles. We three older siblings were not happy about this move, having to leave our friends, entertainment, and a part-time job I had at the dry cleaner. This was our third move in ten years, and each time it was harder to reestablish myself in a new school.

Our family of seven pulled up into the driveway of our new home. It was bigger than the last one, two stories and with a big backyard. I was sixteen then, unloading many boxes with my sister Debby. Butch had his own room, and my two younger sisters shared a room. All bedrooms were upstairs, and our mom and stepdad had their master bedroom downstairs. The neighborhood was quite nice, with fresh new homes that were just built.

While we were all unpacking the cars and the truck that delivered our household furnishings, a teenage girl about my age walked over to introduce herself. "Hi, I'm Kiese." She was so cool—a true Beatnik, brainy and pretty. I replied, "My name is Pat Blanco." I was no longer going by the name "Patty," a name that was too childish for me at that point in my life. "Pat" holds the true meaning of my name: "noble one."

We immediately became good friends. She and nine siblings plus her parents made a family of eleven living in the five-bedroom home next door. They had just moved there a year prior, having come from Washington State.

I was so glad to have Kiese as a friend and to go to the same high school. Starting a new school after spring break was not easy for me—right in in the middle of a semester. I sure had a lot of mean eyes staring at me. But thank God, Kiese met with me during lunchtime and introduced me to her friends. I was feeling pretty good about myself. It was a small school of about 350 sophomores. But that made it easier for me to figure out which groups of people were popular and which ones were not groovy, or should I say, hotheaded.

After a month living in this small town, I was anxious to go out and party, to be where the teens hang out for fun. When I lived in Burbank, I had lots of places to go for entertainment, like a movie theater, dance hall, and spots where teens hang out with their fast cars. "Kiese, where does everyone go for fun?" I asked. She looked at me as if I had asked a serious question. But I insisted that we should go out and have fun! I borrowed my mom's car, and off we went to Dunker's Donut, the hangout of the Dunker's Punkers. This group was classified as "lowriders," driving fast '55 Chevys or Fords and sitting low in their seats as they went cruising the town. As I pulled up to the place, my friend Kiese said, "Wait, are you sure you want to do this?" I said "Yes, and why are you so shy?" I was dressed to kill in my white shorts, called "hot pants" at the time, and white boots. My hair was in a beehive and I had on perfect '60s makeup. I was emulating Nancy Sinatra and her famous song: "These boots are made for walking, and that's just what they'll do. One of these days these boots are gonna walk all over you!" I loved to sing and dance and dress up!

I had the moves, and this was my night to groove through the place. Kiese was Ms. Beatnik, with her straight, dark hair and false eyelashes. We were ready to turn all heads and make history in this town.

As we entered Dunker's Donut, we saw many people our age hanging out and having fun playing the jukebox (old-school coin-operated music system). The classic jukebox has buttons, with letters and numbers on them, which are used to select a specific record to play the hit songs of the '50s and '60s. This group of teens transformed the dowdy Dunker's Donut into a disco "happening."

Roaming around and enjoying myself, I noticed that a good-looking, cool guy was staring at me. He had blond hair and hazel eyes and was irresistibly handsome. After a few minutes, he walked toward me and sat on the chair next to me. He introduced himself, "Hey, I'm Steve." I introduced myself, and we had a long conversation. I don't know how time passed so quickly, as we hit it off instantly. He invited me to check out his fast '55 Chevy. He'd rebuilt the engine for it, to use for drag races. Kiese was introduced to a few of his friends and met a cool guy name Jerry. We were both being accepted as the new girls of Dunker's Punkers.

On our very first dance night a few weeks later, I dressed in my best clothes and met Steve. A large dance hall full of young adults and teens was reveling with laughter, dancing, and chatting. The place was full of love and happiness, and since I loved to dance, it was an evening of great excitement for me. Though Steve was not much of a dancer, having my friend Kiese by my side covered it. While dancing, Steve kept his eyes constantly on me, admiring every inch of me. His eyes revealed that he was falling in love with me with every passing moment. I felt special.

Things were going perfectly for me in this town. There were no school bullies to pull me down for my hearing and speech impairments as in previous schools. I created a new image for myself by pretending that my speech impairment was an accent, like I was a foreigner from Europe. They called me "stuck up" because most of the time I was not able to hear them calling or talking to me from a distance. Sometimes I just kept walking as if I were not interested in becoming their friend. Things at home were also improving because my mom was making progress in saving for her divorce from my stepdad, Mitch. It was so courageous for my mother to do this with five children and no education to fall back on. During the '60s, it was not common to divorce, but my mom stood up for the right thing and decided to live her life free from the abuse and dirty secrets.

During this time, my best friend Kiese and I got jobs at a hamburger stand called Chubby Boys. It was another hangout for boys to meet the pretty girls that worked there. Kiese and I made that place popular with our groovy charm. I also wanted to support my mom in the tough times because she was going through the divorce to save us all from further abuse.

Because I was stress free at school, my grades improved. I kept good company with many good friends and also had two extraordinary people in my life, Kiese and Steve.

One night, Steve took me to the drive-in theatre in town, and we learned a lot about each other. He told me about his family and what they did for a living, and that he worked for a family friend's gas station, building engines and repairing cars.

He told me about his sister, Diane, who was the same age as me, and one day I met her in our history class at school. I believed we got along well, until one day when she and I got into an argument.

I don't recall how the argument developed, but I did know that she didn't want me to be with her brother, Steve. Since she was best friends with Steve's ex-girlfriend, she wanted Steve to leave me and get back with his ex.

The argument quickly escalated to a fight right there in class, and we stood up to hit each other. She punched me in the face, and then I returned the favor. There was a fistfight in the classroom, and all the students were looking at us. I remember the teacher came up to us and tried to separate us. He then sent both of us to the principal's office.

That was the very first time in my life I felt strong. I was defending myself and taking a stand for who I really was, not allowing anyone to degrade me. I had come to the point of no return, leaving behind all the bullying and crying. Years of staying silent and not fighting back strengthened me for this moment. I'd become a woman with backbone!

After a warning from the principal and a list of dos and don'ts, we were both sent home. Despite such a terrible fight, Steve and I remained a couple. He still loved me the way he used to and was still as supportive as ever. He taught me how to drive and let me learn in his '55 Chevy race car.

We went on a drive in that car to a drag race at White Avenue in Pomona, near the LA Fairgrounds. There were other fast cars lined up for a drag race on this highway, as it was a weekly thing for these guys to show off and win popularity points. Today it would be called "Fast and Furious!" Steve even reminds me a lot of Vin Diesel, having the same character.

As he lined up with his competitors, Steve asked me to stay in the car with him as his good-luck charm. The loud mufflers and revving engines made my heart race, as I was about to have the ride of my life! My stomach came up to my chest, and I screamed a shout of victory—a scream that had been suppressed by years of abuse and bullying. Today I can see why those giant roller-coaster rides are so popular. People need the thrill of screaming their guts out from years of suppressed misery. It's something you might want to try, to release those pent-up emotions. "Fast and furious" is too dangerous these days, and getting caught would be jail time.

I had strong feelings for Steve, and I made up my mind that he was the man I was going to marry. He was my first and last love. He was fun, cool, a leader, and he was popular. After all, this is how most of us think as teenagers—that our first love is going to translate into a lifetime of fantasy. But reality holds something completely opposite for us. Things can't always be the way we want them to be. I did give up my virginity at age sixteen. It was not what I expected; I thought it would make him love me more.

I want today's teenagers to understand the fact that sex was created by God for marriage, that you may enjoy each other in commitment and have children together. Teenagers are too young to understand and commit to such pleasure God has given us. Having sex is one thing, and loving someone is another thing. Sex never makes you fall in love. It just feeds the craving of being with someone who can satisfy your sexual desires. I believe sex should be enjoyed with your spouse, the person you are willing to give all your being to. Therefore, this culture of premarital sex should not be encouraged. I would advise all my young readers that you should save yourself for the right mate that God has for you. God knows the hearts of everyone on this planet, and He can save us from a lot of misery.

Getting back to my story—the day after Steve and I were intimate, I got home and went directly into my room. I sat on my bed and started thinking. There was a roller coaster of emotions inside me, and I was wondering whether Steve would marry me or not. I had given myself to him completely, and now I didn't even know if I should have trusted him. But gladly, things were fine after that intimate evening.

Steve and I spent much time together, having the best time of our lives. But then one sad day, I learned that Steve was doing drugs behind my back. As I discussed earlier, I, too, had gotten into drugs because of my friends and the company that I kept. But now, after finding out that yet again I was around drug users, it started haunting me. I recalled those times I saw people being rushed to the hospital for drug overdoses, many losing their lives. I didn't want to live that again. I had tried hard to detach myself from all that and live a drug-free life.

In those days, riots, movements, and protests were taking place because of the Vietnam War. Many young people around the country became increasingly aware of social issues such as war and freedom. They found many causes such as civil rights, anti-war, and anti-censorship to rally behind. Many students protested the Vietnam War, which dragged on until 1975.

Tens of thousands of soldiers lost their lives during this war, and all those families were affected. Billions of dollars were spent to send arms and ammunition to Vietnam and to offer them our support in the war. But this act did not turn out well because the U.S. economy suffered for quite a few years afterward.

But even during those times, most of my friends were like zombies. They outwardly appeared as fine, good-looking people, but inside they were zombies. They were not concerned with the war or social problems their country was facing. Instead, they smoked pot at the park with their hippy friends, singing Dylan, Hendrix, and Grateful Dead songs.

My relationship with Steve began to fade. Because he was into doing drugs and other non-serious things, the future I'd imagined with him became an apparition. It was difficult to be with a man who was indifferent to American current events as well as those around the world—one who only ever cared about drugs and cars. I didn't want the father of my children to be an irresponsible drug addict. I seriously began reconsidering this relationship.

Because of the drug explosion and other unhygienic activities, there was a hepatitis outbreak in the '60s. Just like today, as people are dying of COVID, thousands died then of hepatitis. I remember once we went to Lake Havasu, where a group of people was gathered partying. I noticed people were using drugs and needles and getting very stoned. I knew at the time it was a bad idea and I needed to make some changes. A wine bottle was being passed around, and I drank from it. I contracted hepatitis from that, and I was hospitalized. I remember thinking my life would end at that very moment.

By the age of eighteen, I had ulcers, and the doctor made it clear to me if I did not take care of myself emotionally, I would end up with a lifetime of stomach problems. I knew at that moment that I was done. I hated drugs and everything about them. Luckily, I was able to fight it and come through to the other side.

The drug epidemic got so bad that even my brother, Butch, got caught up in it, and one day we found that he had overdosed. My mother rushed him to the hospital, and by the grace of God, the doctors were able to save him.

This was just the beginning of my brother's rough patches, even though he was only fourteen or fifteen at the time. As mentioned, my stepdad, Mitch, was very abusive to him.

Mitch beat all of us, but my brother most of all. And the more he abused him, the more my brother rebelled. He dropped out of school and even ran away from the house one day, which prompted Mitch to send him to boy's camp.

The more I saw of my brother's circumstance, the more I wanted to leave this town. The more my stepdad became overbearing to his family, the more suffocated I became. My mind kept drifting. I knew I was done. I was tired. I had to leave. This town didn't feel like home anymore.

What helped my process was finally breaking up with my boyfriend. It happened when I once took his '55 Chevy out for a ride. I was listening to the tune, "Born To Be Wild," by Steppenwolf. I was driving down the road, when I was flagged down and stopped by a cop. What could I possibly have done? It turned out that the car muffler was too loud. I was baffled. It was the '60s, and everyone had loud mufflers. I was so confused. In that confusion, I took the ticket that the cop booked me for and went on my way.

When I got home, I told my boyfriend what had happened, and he told me that he would take care of it, and that was that.

Sometime later, my family got a knock on the door, and my mother opened it to find a cop asking for me. He told her that I had an unpaid ticket and had to come down to the station with him. I closed my eyes and sighed, realizing that my boyfriend had not, in fact, dealt with it.

I decided then and there to break up with him and move forward with my life. I was done. I was not "Born To Be Wild!" Life had a better plan for me, and I was turned off by this generation of drugs, heavy-metal music, hippies, civil-rights protesting, Vietnam War killings, the Jesus Movement, and more. I was at the "Valley of the Dolls" stage of my life. If you have never seen the movie, I recommend it. It had a big effect on me, because it dramatizes how people can get caught on the wrong path and end up miserable. The famous actress Sharon Tate did end up in a true-life devastation, murdered during the Charles Manson death spree. These were the type of people that were coming out of this wild generation of the '60s.

With each passing day, the town of La Verne became more and more of a sinking ship to me. It was taking me in a downward spiral, and I hated the idea of being caught up in it for the rest of my life. I had to make some big choices in my life. I knew it would be hard if I wasn't prepared to leave this place, so I started focusing on my studies to improve my grades again. My friend Kiese, the coolest girl who was so nice to me all the time, determined to help me raise my grades.

As I changed my way of doing things and cut certain people out of my life, it felt good to rise up and take control of my life. When we come to a brick wall in our lives, it's time to turn right and not climb over, as misery is waiting for you on the other side. So, I took a right and headed for a new opportunity: the La Verne Beauty Pageant.

It was a positive direction for me but a scary one too. I did not have the confidence to stand on stage and speak before judges and audiences. Kiese rescued me again, helping me overcome stage fright for this pageant. This competition was the best training for me, as it brought discovery of my true talents. Though I liked the idea of dressing up pretty, I still needed my friend to push me.

This event developed my fashion-design and social skills, which I thought could be helpful for my future because I wanted to pursue fashion design.

Kiese had bought a dress for a wedding she'd had to attend, and, being the wonderful person she was, she offered it to me. The gown was red velvet, one of a kind, and fit me perfectly. Now all I needed was to make myself a dress for the interview competition. I made a white satin dress with white chiffon draping over my shoulders. This dress was part of my homemaking class project in school.

I had the looks and the dresses but still needed one important thing—a talent for the competition. At first I was stumped, but then I remembered the 007 Bond movie, *Goldfinger*.

I was always a huge fan of *American Bandstand* and dancing, and I watched many TV shows and films. It was one of my favorite things to do in my spare time—to dance alone with music from the top-ten charts and dream of my future. But I needed a solo to perform in this competition.

Yes! I would choreograph a modern-jazz dance to the *Goldfinger* theme song. Of all the films Sean Connery starred in, this famous James Bond film was a huge favorite of mine. And in that film, the villain covers Jill Masterson in gold paint to kill her. It was an exciting idea. It really appealed to me, so I ran with it. I got a ton of body paint and a leotard body suit for the talent competition. Kiese prepared me by covering my entire body with sparkling gold paint. I looked like the quintessential Bond girl.

When they called out "Pat Blanco," I went onto the stage wearing that gold paint.

The trumpets blared in periodic bursts, as the *Goldfinger* theme song progressed. I started my dance in the middle of the stage, lying on the floor, painted in gold, and as Shirley Bassey's voice filled the auditorium, I quickened the pace of my movements, and the song reached its crescendo. I danced out the whole song. It was a golden moment, the message of my life to come. Hear a few of its lyrics: "Mister Goldfinger. Pretty girl, beware of this heart of gold, his heart is cold! Golden words he will pour in your ear, but his lies can't disguise what you fear. For a golden girl knows when he's kissed her, it's the kiss of death from Mister Goldfinger."

As I finished and the song ended, I came down from the high and looked at the crowd. It seemed like the whole town was there. And they all looked like they had their minds blown away. They applauded as I looked on in amazement at their response. I quickly went backstage and showered. Kiese helped me to get the paint off my body and put on the custom-made red gown and return to present myself to the judges and stand with the other contestants. I was feeling confident and ready to answer my question in the interview competition. I cannot thank Kiese enough for encouraging me back then with tips on how to present myself with a clear, still voice on stage, and for remaining my friend for these fifty-five years. I ended up getting the third spot, which I was completely happy with. The fact that I got into the top three out of all those girls amazed me. It truly was an excellent experience for me, and I felt like it would be the start of a new future. There were more pageants ahead of me that I will share in the upcoming chapters.

Graduation came with a new outlook on life. I made it with good grades, especially in my art classes with Miss May. Other students called me the teacher's pet, maybe because she encouraged me to continue my creative-art pursuits since I was so good at it. My homemaking class consisted of cooking and sewing. The other students admired me for my creativity in designing my own clothing. My family was proud of me and knew that one day I was going to be a hit success in the beauty field.

Just before I turned nineteen, I worked a good job waitressing and saved up money to make my first move. My mother and step-dad divorced, and Mom found a job working at a children's daycare center. I was proud of her for finding new ways to support my siblings. But Butch and Debby had taken a different path than me. We were not so close anymore, as the abuse we suffered left a trail of anger and heartache. Later you will learn more about our differences, choices, devastations, and victories from generation to generation. It was exciting having my own apartment in Pomona, working as a waitress, and having a part time job as a sewing-machine operator. I was meeting news friends and enjoying freedom from the unpleasant lifestyles of small-town La Verne.

Discover Pat's Mindset

PAT MEDITATED ON THE GOOD INSTEAD OF THE BAD IN HER LIFE! SHE WAS NAMED PATRICIA, "NOBLE ONE."

"YOU ARE SPECIAL, AND YOU HAVE TALENTS" (AS SPOKEN BY HER GRANDMOTHER) BECAME A BEACON IN HER HEART.

"YOUR WORD IS A LAMP TO MY FEET AND A LIGHT TO MY PATH." (PSALM 119:105)

Chapter 3

THE '70s: LOOKING FOR A ROLE MODEL

Moving to a new city, Pomona, was a different experience for me because of the new confidence I'd gained from doing the beauty pageant, where I received a standing ovation for the *Goldfinger* dance. This awakened me to step out boldly. It was apropos that such an awakening came just as the "Me" decade took off. The popular, sporty, straight-A students went to college or found great careers. Those that got married right after school continued their careers and college education. Life was full of opportunity for most straight-minded graduates.

Most in the hippie culture went into the health-food business or followed the Jesus Movement. As I mentioned, I didn't identify with that movement, but some great people came out of it. One of the wildest hippies, Jeff Fenholt (star of the Broadway musical *Jesus Christ Superstar*) became one of my dear friends in the '90s. Working my job as a sewing-machine operator during the week and cocktail waitressing on the weekends was going quite well for me as I continued searching for a good role model in my life. I gained a spirit of independence, working and supporting myself and making friends. My closest friend was a girl by the name of Noela. She was just about my age and worked in the same bar. She loved to bar-hop whenever possible.

I had left La Verne to progress further along the adventurous path of my life but still longed for external inspiration—a role model, an ideal to strive toward.

Those role models of yesteryear I'd left back in the '60s. They'd all disappointed me with their dark-sided drug addiction. I left that world behind forever.

Life became a whirlwind quite soon after I was offered the job of waitressing at the Ontario Motor Speedway.

Steve, the boyfriend from high school, raced cool cars, and my time with him had imbued me with a passion for cars. Though I knew I would be remote from the cars, I had to take this job. It was unforgettable!

At the Speedway I met and instantly connected with a man named James. Before I knew it, we were hanging out as boyfriend and girlfriend.

I had to be with him, and he had to be with me. He introduced me to the guys down in the pits, where I met the drivers and sat in some of the cars. It was a thrill because these cars were insane, basically built like Indy 500 roadsters that raced like bullets down the track.

James and I were constantly together, but there was a little hitch in the plan. He lived in Hawaii. To him, the solution was easy: come to Hawaii to visit him. I wasn't sure what to do; I wanted to go to Hawaii and always wanted to travel. Who doesn't? But I was a bit nervous and wary.

Still, my heart was telling me to go. When I told my friend about this, she was so excited. She told me to "go immediately." I laughed and calmed her down. By the time I hung up, I'd made up my mind. I was going to Hawaii.

It took forever to find the time to arrange it—an excruciatingly long month. But I finally packed my bags and headed to the airport. I headed to Hawaii via the new Pan American World Airline Boeing 747 to meet my boyfriend. What an opportune adventure to fly on the biggest luxury airline. Life was *good.*

The moment I landed in Hawaii, I fell in love with it, so much so that I decided to stay after exploring it for just a few days.

I wanted an apartment, and as luck would have it, James knew two girls searching for an apartment also. We met and they seemed amiable, thus the decision was made. I was going to live in Hawaii in a comfortable apartment with friends.

I was living life in the fast lane as a twenty-year-old in Hawaii, working three jobs and enjoying independence. One job was as a cocktail waitress, the second as a go-go dancer, and the third one as a barkeeper trainee.

I always felt that if you get an opportunity to move forward, to do something big or to travel to another country, do it. I also had the "power-through" mentality. I have never been held down or held back, never cared if I had past trauma or issues. I would always shove them down and do whatever I wanted. I was propelled by the words of my grandmother: "*You are special*."

Life is like a box of chocolates. You never know what you're going to get. Hawaii was just like that—meeting people from all over the world and finding some not so pleasant and others a real treat!

One of my "treats" (namely James) came to a hard and fast breakup. He was involved in the homosexual lifestyle, which came as a shock to me. I never knew any homosexual people, so it was strange to know my boyfriend was involved in that lifestyle. He was also interested in swinging.

I didn't have a problem with his sexuality, but it was still a bit jarring, and his swinger lifestyle definitely did not agree with me. It was over. But the whirlwind of different opportunities continued; I was quickly scouted by a man who wanted me to be a product model at his convention. I took this exciting offer and worked the convention for a little while. While at my vendor table, a handsome man approached me. It was the actor Frankie Avalon! He was the guy who starred in the beach-party movies and *Grease*. I swooned.

We went out a few times, but it did not last long. He'd pick me up in a limousine and take me to fancy restaurants, and by the time his attraction was over, we were too. That's how these famous people were. They tried someone on, and if they weren't the right "size," they were dropped. Not that I'm complaining—Frankie was a total gentleman, and we had delightful times during our brief time together. And it was nice to experience the celebrity lifestyle, brief as it was.

Hawaii had become a life of short conversations, eating, and drinking, but no solid relationships to build a future for myself or my career. It felt like I was on an endless vacation and needed to get back to my life goals. Life took me back to my home state of California soon enough, where I found an apartment with some girlfriends.

A friend of mine worked at the *Let's Make a Deal* studio show and mentioned that I would be a great candidate for the show. I leapt at the idea and created a Hawaiian costume with leis that looked real. My Hawaiian dance got their attention, and they chose me. WOW! I won the first prize, which was a TV and recliner chair, but turned it in for the chance to win the big deal or big door. Guess what? I won the Big Deal! A trip to Europe, luggage, and cash! I will share later why it took me three years to take the trip.

With the '70s came a new era and with it a new trend. The rise of disco in the 1970s had an enormous cultural impact on the American audience. It was the music heard on the radio, the music everyone danced to. It had connections to R&B and funk, but it was also born of the urban gay culture in New York City. All my girlfriends were raving about it, so off we went to the discotheques in our disco apparel. The music, the flashing lights, the writhing sweaty bodies! It was peak '70s. Like a scene out of *Saturday Night Fever*, I met my first husband at a disco. Ron Sherburne was from a very well-to-do family, and even better, he shared my interests. He genuinely took interest in the things that interested me, and he quickly became the man that I was comfortable with. I could see myself spending my life with him.

He was also a car salesman, which matched up perfectly with my love of cars and drag racing. To this day, I still love fast, sporty cars, and I sometimes speed through empty highways.

We shared comfortable time together, but just as I was settling back into California, he wanted to move to Nevada. Las Vegas, to be exact. His aunt was there, and he believed he could easily get a job there in the auto industry. Since I had some experience in that industry, he felt it was a good fit.

This presented yet another big move, but I was going with the flow of life and wasn't bothered. I agreed to the move and got a job as a cocktail waitress at the Hilton Hotel. That was funny because I'd had a job at the Hilton Hotel in Hawaii as a cocktail waitress. It seemed like life was determined to pull me in one direction.

Ron was very athletic, playing all sports, especially tennis. I had the luxury of learning tennis and golf while in Vegas. We also dined in the most luxurious restaurants. My highlight in Vegas was seeing Elvis Presley on stage from a second-row seat. What a legendary performer—a legend that still touches many a heart and soul today.

Unbeknownst to me at the time, Ron was the nephew of Pancho Gonzalez, the famous tennis player of that era. Many athletes and entertainment legends made Vegas the ultimate place of escape.

Working there, I saw movies being filmed in Vegas all the time. By sheer chance, I was offered a minor speaking role in a movie. I was overjoyed and so ready to do it. Then I discovered, by peeing on a stick, that I had life growing inside me.

I immediately told Ron, of course, and he was taken aback. I wondered if he would do the right thing, like my father had done with my mother. He took me to a nice dinner and proposed to me a few days later. I was shocked, but I agreed. Robert always did have the charm and the charisma to get people to do whatever he wanted.

We moved back to California because his parents were supportive of us, giving us a down-payment for a beautiful home in the city of Diamond Bar. My Happy Days had arrived! Like my father, Ron gave me the best days of my life by providing a loving and safe home environment.

Mr. and Mrs. Robert and Carolynn Sherburne became my father- and mother-in-law, and they were proud to have their first granddaughter. I then realized what kind of family this was. They weren't just well-off; they were lavish, flying us to Palm Springs in their private jet for family gatherings.

Robert ("Bob," as he liked being called) was a successful businessman and a wonderful gentleman who enjoyed being with his family of three and now his new granddaughter. I was thankful that my baby would grow up comfortably. Or so I thought.

Seven months later I had a full belly. I began noticing that my husband, Ron, was working longer hours than normal. I suspected he was cheating. That is one of the first places a woman's mind goes.

My suspicions were confirmed when I walked into a bar one day and saw him chatting with another woman. I walked up, grabbed a glass of water, and threw it at his face. I told him not to bother to come home because we were finished. It's very emotional to have an unfaithful mate and be pregnant at the same time.

Some women feel that it is their appearance, having a big belly and extra weight, that turns men to seek other women. That is not always the case, because some men find a pregnant woman more beautiful, for there is a glow that shines through her while another life is being developed with God's marvelous creativity.

Time passed, and I gave birth. I was soon blessed with a beautiful daughter whose name is Shawna Jean Sherburne. This seven-pound, four-ounce girl was a very healthy ball of joy! She was my life and my angel; I had a big photoshoot with her after the birth. I wanted her to be the next model for baby commercials. I got started getting her into show business by bringing her into small commercials and print work from a very young age. I wanted her to reach every height she could.

Times got a bit tense soon thereafter; my savings had been good but began to thin out. I had to get a job to provide for my daughter, since I was about to separate from Ron, her father.

One day, I went to the bar with my girlfriends, and a man "discovered" me, saying he worked with a modeling agency called Fontaine Modeling Agency. "You seem the type that this agency would represent." Now I finally found my role models, like Cristina Ferrare, the Max Factor Cosmetic face model. Other similar styles of models were Jacqueline Smith of *Charlie's Angels* and my favorite, Wonder Woman (Lynda Carter).

I took a job at a place called Jack LaLanne European Health Club. It was wonderful and the most stable workplace of my life. The place was run by a woman named Nancy Baker and her two daughters.

Nancy is one of the most beautiful people I've ever met, and I was surprised to find she was religious. Her Christianity was the most spiritual I'd ever experienced. I grew up Catholic, and the only religious environment I'd known was sober and strict. This woman's Christian lifestyle and values made me wish I had been born into her sort of religious environment. Nancy wasn't favorable toward the California culture of that time. When I took her out to a disco one time, she disliked it. She only disclosed this to me *years* after that event, but she hated going to that place. She despised how everyone sought temporary solace in the hookup culture. She was quite the spiritual person and told me she could see through everyone there, and that the place reeked of loneliness. My separation from Ron made it harder for me to find babysitters for my Shawna. I needed to find someone I could trust to care for her while I developed my career. I had a good relationship with my ex-in-laws Robert and Carolynn, who loved and adored their granddaughter. They were sad that their son's marriage was failing, but their love for Shawna and care for me overrode that sadness.

I later signed a contract with La Fontaine Modeling Agency and modeled for them on a part-time basis, as the work was touch and go—not an income I could count on. I added to it with a waitress job and became a car salesperson, which was something I loved doing. Life became full, taking care of my daughter, modeling, and going out with friends. However, I had much more in store for me.

Now the time came for me to take the *Let's Make a Deal* prize. I had won the trip to Europe, and now I found a girlfriend to take this trip with me. It was the journey of a lifetime. God gave me the courage to take this trip alone for the first five days and then meet up with my girlfriend in Germany. I had a list of people to visit who lived in Germany, Italy, and London. As a model, I met people from different parts of the world, and when I lived in Vegas, I met even more. I was good at keeping connected with people. My first stop was an overnight in Switzerland. It was like a fairytale country full of the most beautiful flowers and villages. I met a young Swiss man on the plane, and he invited me to stay at his parents' home. God certainly gave me favor from one person to another in each country as I took this three-week trip by Eurail train. My friend Carol and I also met so many Americans. As Americans we are very blessed. Though Europe has its history, beauty, and hospitality, it is still not America, the land of the free. After visiting Europe, I was able to truly appreciate the Bicentennial, the 200th anniversary of Independence Day, celebrated on Sunday, July 4, 1976.

I lived in a generation that witnessed the good, the bad, and the ugly. Does anyone remember some of the '70s' most memorable incidents that took place in our country and changed history? Like 100,000 people in Washington, D.C., demonstrating against the Vietnam War? Or the Watergate scandal, in which five men broke into the Democratic National Committee headquarters? President Richard Nixon was the first president to resign and remains the only one to this day. And the most tragic was the Jonestown Massacre led by Jim Jones! Nine hundred cult members were induced to drink a deadly poison.

Awakenings were still happening through it all, just like today's generation, as a wakeup call to get right with God and yourself. My life was so busy that I had no time available for my daughter, which caused her grandparents to become resentful of me. They had hoped I would still be a part of their daily life along with their son, Ron, but because of his sex addiction, I saw no future with him. We are all responsible for our actions, and as we make difficult decisions in our life, there are consequences. Forgiveness is the key to get through life's hardships and start a new life on a clean slate. I will share more about this in the next chapter.

I began to focus even more on my career. After being promoted to manager of the Jack LaLanne Spa, I met a gentleman who was opening another health club and was adding a skincare salon to his facility. This was something that held great interest for me because my skin looked great, and I used many beauty tips to keep my skin ageless and glowing. I was sent to the Elegante Beauty School for six months to get my license as an esthetician and beauty consultant. It was all paid for by this gentleman who saw my potential to make it big in the skincare-beauty industry.

After finishing beauty school, his offer regarding the new health spa evaporated due to bankruptcy during the building of his new business. But that event did not stop me from moving forward in my career as a beauty consultant, for I was determined to make it happen elsewhere. All the doors were about to open as I made a new move to Cheviot Hills, a city near Beverly Hills, with my friend Noela. I was living in the midst of Hollywood glamour, salons, private nightclubs, and fancy parties. This part of town was full of beautiful people looking for stardom. I was close to my modeling agency and still going out on interviews.

One interview was for the Miss Catalina Pageant. Catalina is a small island off the coast of California that many of the locals in Los Angeles County would visit to get away and relax. So, another opportunity to compete and win a new platform in the big city of L.A.

This was my first trip to the island, competing with fifty ladies to win the crown. I had already known the discipline it takes to win, and now it was up to the judges to pick their favorite. I did not win this pageant but had an amazing experience meeting people in the entertainment field, which inspired me to move forward with my gifts and talents.

Now my focus was on opening a skincare salon. I had my certifications and resume full of experience that was impressive. I had done much makeup, hair, and fashion styling over the years as an independent beauty consultant. Remember, I was a natural with this even at the early age of fifteen. My makeup/stylist portfolio was looking good, and doors opened with many photographers who liked my work.

To be successful in this business it was all about who you know. As you may have surmised by now, I was not shy and found ways to meet the right people to take my career to the next level. I found another man who invested in my plans to open a skincare/ makeup studio in the famous beauty salon called Saul's in Marina Del Rey.

Yes! This was my big break. And a high-rise penthouse apartment went with it, right on the beach. This became another, but much more conducive, move toward my dream. Life was getting so exciting, and I was doing what I loved the most: making women feel and look beautiful.

Within two years, I had opened three skincare rooms with full treatments for body and makeup. Plus, I was introduced to the head makeup artist at the ABC Entertainment Center in Century City. I had a room in that center with a lot of people from ABC Corp.

Life was rolling with the money and fame, from dance competitions to invitations to Hollywood parties. I became my own role model! But I must say, I learned from the pros by studying what they did to keep their beauty and stay in shape for the fame.

My daughter Shawna joined me on a few modeling shoots. New career with the Fontaine Modeling Agency.

Discover Trish's Mindset

TRISH STAYED FOCUSED ON HER GIFTS AND STEPPED OUT IN FAITH. TRISH'S CHRISTIAN FRIEND NANCY BAKER HAD BEEN PRAYING FOR HER IN SECRET FOR YEARS. IS THERE SOMEONE YOU KNOW THAT NEEDS PRAYER?

"CONFESS YOUR TRESPASSES TO ONE ANOTHER, AND PRAY FOR ONE ANOTHER, THAT YOU MAY BE HEALED. THE EFFECTIVE, FERVENT PRAYER OF A RIGHTEOUS WOMAN AVAILS MUCH. (JAMES 5:16)

Trish was being discovered as a beauty expert through many known photographers.

Chapter 4

The '80s: What In The World Happened?

The turn of the decade brought about a lot of changes for me, both personal and social. The '80s decade came, and it seemed that the media industry transformed itself overnight. New styles, new trends, new technology, a whole new environment. I also had made a lot of progress: I now had my own business and worked as a make-up artist, wardrobe stylist, model, and beauty consultant. I had always dreamed of this. Even when I was at school in my early teens, I always picked the role of fashion designer, and I excelled in my art classes. It was my passion, and I could not have been happier that I was now pursuing it.

With the new decade, the New-Wave era arrived, and Hollywood was revolutionized. It was the age of innovation and color—so much color. Every movie was flashy and bright and had a completely different vibe. During that era, we also saw incredible movies about dance and entertainment.

And as you know, dancing was my dream. The song from the film *Flashdance*, called "What a Feeling," brought out the boldest dance in a unique way. I couldn't count the times I listened to and danced to that song. It just had that feeling to it that you could not stop dancing.

And so a wave had begun. Dancing in the nightclubs became choreographed. With some contacts I had built, I got a chance to start choreographing those dances to include the fashions of the '80s at the nightclubs. It felt like a dream. I instructed the dancers, and they went out on the stage every night and did what I showed them. The world saw my talent and my craft in the arts of fashion and dance.

Life was thriving for me in my business, I was following my passion, and it felt amazing. But there was a part of me that felt empty—that felt lonely in my penthouse apartment overlooking the beach. I was missing my daughter Shawna, who had been raised by her grandparents for the past three years due to my busy lifestyle.

It seemed that someone was listening. One day I went to Pier 1 Imports in Marina Del Rey, where I was living in a very nice penthouse apartment.

I went into the place to buy some roller skates. I was an avid dancer, but I also quite liked roller skating. Gliding over the floor in simple but graceful movements was relaxing, and I had to buy them. When I went in, I heard a couple of men standing to the side. They seemed to have noticed me, and I knew they would approach. And when I got in line, one of them quickly came and stood behind me, a tactic I had seen used a thousand times before.

He asked me if I was buying the skates to compete in the roller derby. A silly question that I scoffed at. I told him no, I was just buying the skates to go on the beach bike and skate path that ran from Marina Del Rey to Muscle Beach in Venice.

He thought it was cool. He introduced himself as Peter and asked me to go to lunch on the beach with him. He was nice and charming, so I thought, "What the heck?" and told him yes.

We met up later for lunch on the beach and had our first date. He told me about himself. The impression I got was that he was a conservative and successful businessman and father of an eleven-year-old daughter.

I thought perhaps it was time to settle down with someone more mature. My past relationships hadn't exactly been great, so I made a decision.

We moved quickly in the relationship. He soon asked me to move in with him, which I did, leaving my penthouse apartment. An important thing about him was that he had a daughter. And since I had a daughter who had been living with her grandparents, I thought it would be a perfect time to have her live with me. Peter's daughter and my daughter could grow up together, and it would be a perfect family for us all!

There were problems with this plan, of course. I had to explain the soon-to-be-ex-husband thing, as I was still married. The divorce proceedings were going to be expensive, and I knew it was going to be complicated as well, so Ron and I had just stayed separated. That became a problem when Peter wanted us to marry, but he understood and helped me with the proceedings. It took some time and a lot of money.

The first problem was that Shawna's father had decided to litigate to pursue custody over her. Also, Robert and Carolynn Sherburne (his parents) had hired an attorney because they also wanted custody. The fight was going to be intense, with two attorneys fighting for custody of my daughter.

I fought that legal battle for a long time before I could come to a compromise with Shawna's grandparents. Neither Shawna nor I hated them, and I wanted Shawna to have a relationship with them—to have her grandparents around her.

Only Ron was left to deal with. It was easy to win the case against Ron because all I had to do was prove his bachelor lifestyle was not conducive to raising a child. Shawna's grandparents had withdrawn their support, and I soon won the case. Ron and I were divorced.

But life was hardly sunshine and daisies from there. I didn't perceive it at the time, but Peter was slowly starting to take over my life, becoming controlling and emotionally abusive. It started with him drawing me away from my friends and social life. I started staying in, and then the emotional abuse and arguments began.

There was an incident where I locked myself in my daughter's room after a huge argument, and he kept banging on the door to make me come out. I feared what he might do to me and my daughter.

I'd hoped Peter, our two daughters, and I could become a good family, but those hopes were dashed. He buried those hopes further one day when we were at a bar with friends. Peter was a heavy drinker—as in closing-down-the-bar kind of drinker.

Usually I tolerated it, but I wanted to go home that day. But his friends said, "Let's go to our house." They knew that we were in no condition to be alone, as they had seen for themselves the temper Peter had.

We arrived at our friends' home in Pacific Palisades and jumped in their hot jacuzzi, hoping the alcohol would wear off. The four of us were chatting and having a few laughs, when Peter made an inappropriate sexual demand in that mixed company. I replied with a strong No. His face began to turn red, and a violent action seemed imminent.

I barely saw the punch coming. Yes, a full-fisted punch came my way, and I put my hand up to defend myself instinctively. I forgot that I had a wine glass in my hand. His hand hit my hand, and the wine glass hit my head and shattered. It shattered like my heart, which had been so full of hope for our future.

I was bleeding and quickly got up and out of the jacuzzi and headed to the bathroom. I took one look at myself and heard a voice within me say, “Get out now!” I knew this was my chance, my divine moment to escape this abusive relationship.

I took his car and went to a friend’s house. I asked if she would let me stay with her indefinitely because Peter and I were over. She looked at my wound and intuited what had happened, and quickly told me I could stay as long as I wanted.

I went to the hospital feeling like I was in the twilight zone. The hospital was oddly empty. There was only the receptionist and me. She looked at my appearance, and at first I thought she might ask questions, but she remained quiet and led me to the doctor. I swear that in my life, if I could say that anyone was heaven sent, it would be two people: my darling Shawna and this doctor who helped me.

This doctor was the most compassionate and kind man I had ever met, and he radiated an aura that made me think that everything would be alright. I did now know it at the time, but meeting this man was going to be life changing.

My life was going to move in a wholly different and good direction from then on. He just looked at my wound and told me, “I’m going to fix this. And it’ll be like it never happened.” And I trusted him instantly. I felt safe. I got my treatment, and I was surprised when they told me it was free of charge. They did not even bill me.

I went to my friend's house and dropped my stuff, and I grabbed what little sleep I could that night. In the morning, I got up and went to Shawna's grandparents to pick her up. I hid the bandage on my forehead with a hat.

Shawna already suspected something bad with our relationship, knowing Peter had a temper. I told Shawna, "We are not going back to Peter's house and will be staying with some friends." All our belongings were still there at his house, and I told her that at the right time all of our things would be moved out.

God was taking over my life from this point forward, and my new journey was taking a radical turn. Life is like a roller coaster with ups and downs and merry-go-rounds!

If you are in an abusive relationship, get out! Break the cycle and take a step of faith to a heavenly experience that is waiting for you, to give you a new life.

This is just what Aretha Franklin did in her life in leaving her abuser. I recently saw her life story in the movie called *Respect.* She wrote her story in a song called "Think." Yeah freedom, freedom from the cycle of mind games, manipulations, and violence.

At this time, I began my recovery. I had to start from scratch. My social life had shriveled up after being with Peter for three long years. My reputation had faded. My business was gone due to the changes I'd made while in the relationship with Peter.

It took the next six months to revive all that. Fixing it and making it better would take longer. But I did not give up—I was not that kind of person. I got back into nightclub dance choreography with what little contacts I had left. I revved up my beauty, makeup, and styling business again.

It took a lot of blood, sweat, and tears, but I was not about to let all that I had built over the years just go to waste. I was strong. Life had made me that way. And I would be all that I was meant to be again.

Healing is so important. When you've been through abuse like I have, you need to take a step back, look at yourself, and recognize and understand those signs of abuse. Because if you don't, you will regret it and fall back into that cycle. That is what I did with Peter, a man that I soon realized resembled my stepfather so starkly.

I had to work on that. And I did, by a divine appointment with someone at the Sports Connection Health Club in Santa Monica. God works in mysterious ways, and it can happen to anyone who says, "I need help, God. Where are You?"

A very angelic man jumped onto the cycle machine next to me and began a simple conversation, which led to an invitation to a Bible study. "What is that?" I wondered to myself. But it did not matter, I just knew I had to go to this person's home for a Bible study.

Two days later, my daughter Shawna and I walked into the beautiful Beverly Hills home where the Bible study took place. The moment I walked in I felt the most incredible love and welcoming. I saw the man that invited me and my daughter, and he seated us with a big angelic smile. Within ten minutes, a gentleman and his wife came walking into their living room with a big welcome. There was an opening prayer, and the musician Al Kasha began to sing and play Christian songs I had never heard before. The style of the music was heavenly. It was brought to my attention that evening that Al Kasha was a famous Academy Award–winning composer and songwriter on many films.

Next, I was invited to a Christian church just blocks away from where I was living in Westwood. I had no idea that God's presence dwelled in high school auditoriums. This place was called the Hiding Place. Pastors Henry and Nona Cutrona were young—in their thirties—a cross between hippies and Hollywood stars. Pastor Henry was an excellent guitarist, singer, and preacher.

All the people in this auditorium-church had a radiant glow on their faces. I felt a heavenly atmosphere of love and acceptance, just as I had felt when I first walked into Al Kasha's home. My daughter was with me, and she enjoyed it too.

My healing began every Sunday at this Hiding Place Church, which truly was a hiding place for people to come and heal. A lot of those that attended this church worked in the entertainment industry, so I fit right in! I was meeting like-minded people and hearing their stories of God's miracles, healings, and born-again experiences.

Some of my closest friends today all went to this Hiding Place, and thirty-six years later we still gather. These include my beloved friends Amy Chinian, Lee Benton, Tyra McNamara, Tom Arbia, Joji Pollock, and more.

Six months later, I was at a private nightclub called Vala with my girlfriends. It was one of those new and trendy discos, the happening place in West Hollywood. And it had those long mirrors behind the bar. Now I know why bars have mirrors like that, but at the time I had no idea. I was there drinking when I saw a guy looking at me. He was handsome—as in John Travolta in *Saturday Night Fever* handsome. Swoon-worthy, really.

He was shooting glances at me. When I looked at him in the mirror, he looked away, and when I looked away, I could see through my peripherals that he was looking at me.

It was a shy sort of affair. And maybe I felt ready to dive back into the scene. But first, I went to the restroom to freshen up. When I came back out, I saw him wag his finger at me to call me over. "*Bold!*" I thought.

I went over and said hi. He had a charm in his voice when he talked. The first words out of his mouth were, "Are you busy tonight?" I looked at him with amusement, for he had noticed earlier that I was sitting with some friends and a few men at the bar, but that did not matter to him. He was very confident to steal me away from my group of friends that evening. I replied, "Yes, as you can see, I have company."

"Oh, that's too bad," he said, and I replied, "Do you have a card?" Right then, he handed me over his card, and I noticed his name and title. Jamal Haddad—Photographer.

He had a quality of both swagger and arrogance—incredibly attractive, with thick black hair and nice physique, and he was dressed in the white John Travolta disco suit.

I called him two days later. His first words when he answered were, "I knew you would call." I laughed and realized this guy was full of himself, with an attitude that whatever he wanted, he would definitely get. Jamal asked me to meet him for dinner that weekend.

We met at Jimmy's Restaurant in Beverly Hills, which was the fanciest restaurant in town. I was thirty minutes late due to the lateness of the babysitter.

When I walked in, Jamal was sitting at the bar waiting for me, and the first words out of his mouth were, "You're late." I smiled and shared that my babysitter was late. This let him know that I did have responsibility for a child, but that did not change his plans; he was out to have a romantic evening.

We talked and talked and talked. I told him about my passion for the fashion industry, modeling, and dancing, and he told me about his love of photography. I was enjoying the evening, and many ideas were running through my mind and heart.

We talked about our contacts and realized we could explore our passions together and connect with each other professionally. I asked him if he could photograph models for my makeup/fashion portfolio, and he seemed quite happy to do so. And then I ventured further and asked if he would like to photograph me.

Since I was still attached to Judith Fontaine Modeling Agency, I wanted to continue modeling. He happily agreed. It was a whirlwind romance, and we lost ourselves in it. We spent our days talking about our shared passions and having fun.

Jamal had a very heavy accent when we first met, and I still had my hearing loss. After two months of dating, he felt that our relationship was lacking clarity in our conversations. He asked my roommate Vicki if she could understand him when he spoke. Vicki replied Yes! Then Jamal proceeded with, "Why does Trish have trouble understanding me?" She replied, "Why don't you ask her?"

An evening came when Jamal and I were just hanging out at my apartment in Westwood and having a glass of wine. He asked me, "Do you have a hard time understanding me?" I looked down and began to fear rejection, as I tried to muster enough courage to share the truth about my fake accent, which was actually a speech impediment from my hearing loss. "Remember, Patty, *you are special.*" Those words were ringing in my ears again. Plus, by then I was a very successful woman, and my life was more than trying to be perfect. I finally gathered my thoughts to share the true story of what happened to me as a little girl with a high fever and shortly after that, the trauma of my father's sudden death.

Jamal looked at me with a face of compassion and said, "You are number one! No one should make you feel any less and you should be proud of yourself!" I was so amazed at his reaction to my story that I did feel very special.

What I did not know about Jamal was that underneath all his great looks, playboy personality, and confidence, he planned to end our relationship. But first he wanted to build me up to be strong, so the next person that came along would not be able to hurt me. Well, that all changed, and we ended up staying together for the next three years.

In those three years of dating, we accomplished so much together. I want to point out the divine episodes of our life together, even though I was a lady that knew how to have fun, build a business, and meet the rich and famous.

Episode #1 – Inviting Jamal to the Hiding Place. He felt very uncomfortable due to everyone being so friendly and wanting to hug. He was raised in a Catholic church, and people did not do that. Plus, he was thinking, "What is this long-haired guy doing singing and playing music with a group of hippies and preaching about God? Hey, I am from the Holy Land—Jordan! And what do these freaks know about God?"

Episode #2 – Meeting the Haddad family. Jamal came from a family of eleven, and Arabic language was spoken most of the time, so I was not able to converse in the family gatherings. Jamal was doing all the talking for me. And this family was loud, dramatic, and had their personal secrets that would have made a great TV comedy series.

Episode #3 – We became famous in the disco clubs, and everyone wanted to work for us as models, dancers, and actors. So, we started Steele Productions to help people by placing them in fashion and dance shows at the clubs.

Episode #4 – One more beauty pageant. As you know, *Goldfinger* had helped me to move forward and win a crown. I won the California Gold Coast Pageant as the first runner up of Beauties of America, competing with fifty state winners on the Princess Cruise. Jamal helped me get myself in shape and was so proud of me.

Episode #5 – Jamal Haddad changed his name to Jim Steele. I knew that his name was too Arabic for the film industry, so Jim converted his name to simple English meanings. Jamal to Jim and Haddad to Steele (Haddad means steel worker in Arabic). It was a perfect fit, and it became his legal name when he applied for his citizenship. At the Immigration Office, waiting in line wearing his mafia suit from the movie set that day, the gentleman behind the counter said, "Wow, you look like a movie star!" Jamal replied, "I just came from the movie set." The man said, "Can I have your autograph for my girlfriend?" Jamal replied, "Yes, I have some photos in my briefcase." The man was star-crossed and asked if Jamal wanted to change his name legally. He was immediately given the name Jim Steele.

Episode #6 – I left my apartment in Westwood and moved closer to Jim in Glendale. Within two weeks, he had moved in with me. It was a hard transition due to him being so special to his parents; they lived one mile away from us. But God had a plan. He assured us that we were called to be together, but not to live together.

One day Jim and I had a big argument, and he said he was leaving. As he was walking toward the door something made me jump up and run to him at the door to say, "Wait! Don't leave, God sent you to me!"

We both felt another voice speaking through me; it was the Spirit of God waking us up to get right with Jesus, who was calling us to a born-again experience.

During our first three years of dating, I was still going to church on Sundays because I found a special acceptance that was healing my heart from the past rejections and pain.

One Thursday evening, Pastor Henry was having a healing service for the first time. I felt so compelled to go that evening. Jim and I both wanted to experience a miracle: for my ears to open. At the service, Henry began to teach from different stories in the Bible of how Jesus healed those who came to Him. As he finished his sermon, he said that if anyone needed a healing, they should come to the front and he would lay hands on them for a miracle. I took my walk of faith to the front and believed deeply that Jesus would touch me. Yes! I got my miracle! My ears were opened to hear everything.

That was the most amazing night of my life! Jesus touched me through the hands of Pastor Henry Cutrona. And when I left the church, I stayed overnight at my friend Tyra's home, as she lived close to the Culver City studios where I had to do makeup for an actor on the set.

Jesus was not done with me, and He gave me the gift of speaking in tongues as Tyra laid hands on me. It was a beautiful, heavenly singing language from the Holy Spirit.

Jim went home that night after the healing service with Pastor Henry and had a very unusual experience. He had gone to the front to agree for my healing, and while he was up there, God showed him a vision of him being translated, or transported, into a dark hole—going faster than the speed of light—and it was hellish. Jim was screaming in his mind, "Please don't send me there! Just give me a little place in heaven."

Then the Spirit spoke back to him, saying, "I was not sending you there but showing you that hell is real." Jim did not believe there was a hell, but God wanted to show him because this is why Jesus died for us—to save us from hell.

Now the time came for Jim and me to make some serious decisions in our life together. I knew that I needed to stop living in sin, in a lustful relationship, and to try to serve Jesus instead. I still felt emptiness, and every time Jim and I had sex, I would feel guilty, knowing that Jesus wanted me to give up my lifestyle with Jim and turn to a new life with Him.

An announcement was made at the church that all the singles were invited to a camping trip at Big Bear. It was a three-day trip to be in the presence of God on the mountaintop, an opportunity to have a Moses transformation experience. I was so excited to hear about this that I bought three tickets, for me, my daughter, Shawna, and for Jim.

I shared with Jim that this trip was for all of us to have an amazing time together. Even though I was never the camping type of girl, I knew it was going to be divine. Jim's reaction was, "No, I am not going up there to sleep in tents with a bunch of men who just might be gay." This was his way of getting out of having to go, because he just was not ready to have a born-again experience. He was the ultimate playboy.

I was not about to let Jim's sex life stop me from finding a new life with Jesus. I packed my suitcase and took my daughter and my best friend, Noela, for the four-hour drive to the campgrounds at Big Bear. I was glad to see my new friends, Amy Kellinger and Tyra. It was summertime, and the weather was perfect when we arrived. We met many other singles from the church.

I will always mark these dates, July 15–17, 1988—a time like never before, having my name written in the Book of Life! I had another miracle healing that turned all my sinful self into a person who had no regrets for all I had gone through from childhood until then. I was baptized in the Holy Spirit and fire to serve God with all my heart.

On July 17, 1988, I came home glowing with such confidence and happiness that people could see something had changed in my appearance. When Jim asked how the trip went, I said to him, "I am serving God 100 percent, and you need to move all of your belongings out of the master bedroom into the second room. No more sex, no more living together; you have thirty days to find another place."

Jim was shocked to hear this come out of my mouth because he was my god. I would give in to his charm every time, even when he knew that my lifestyle with him was not satisfying. Jim was seeing another woman while I was in Big Bear, which was revealed to me much later in our journey.

Now, the story gets even more intense and full of unusual events. Let me put them into episodes again. When you make a commitment to serve God 100 percent, you take on a whole new journey that makes you feel like Wonder Woman or Indiana Jones.

Episode #7 – I got invited to many Bible fellowships during the week and became unusually happy. Jim was thinking I must have met another man up in Big Bear. The truth is—yes! Jesus!

Episode #8 – Jim was seeing a new woman, but in his heart, he missed me and hoped to sit and talk about what had happened to me in Big Bear. I had not shared with him the whole story of my amazing born-again experience.

Episode #9 – The last week of that month, in a dream, Jim was taken out of his body again and was translated to the place where Jesus was crucified on the cross. He saw all the people standing around, mocking the man on the cross. Jim asked himself, "What am I doing here?" The man on the cross took one look at Jim and without saying anything, knew everything about Jim. Wow! Jim felt naked and ashamed, for Jesus knew all his secrets. Jim woke up and came back into his body, knowing that this dream was real and needed an interpretation.

Episode #10 – Jim went to his father's house for breakfast that morning, and his father, Aref, looked worried. Jim asked, "What's going on?" His father said, "I saw Jesus last night in my dream, and he gave me a ring that did not fit my finger. He knows my ring size, so why did he give me this ring that does not fit?" Aref came to realize that a ring represents a son, and God gave him a son that did not fit his hand. "One of my four sons is not obeying me, and I have no control over his life."

Episode #11 – That same day, Jim went to see his aunt, a faithful woman of prayer, especially for the Catholic church. Jim told her his dream, and his aunt interpreted it. "You have been living in sin with all these women, and your lifestyle is crucifying Jesus over again. You say you know God, and He has sent you Trish, who is a good woman. You should marry her and stop crucifying Jesus."

By this time, Jim wanted to go back to the Hiding Place on his own. He was still looking for answers, for he knew his lifestyle was not fulfilling but empty. He asked me where the church was. I answered, "If you are going, don't do it for me—do it for Jesus." He got mad at me and decided to go on his own, trying to remember from months prior where this place was. I was always the one that drove him to church when he still had a hangover from the night before in the disco clubs.

Finding the place thirty minutes after the service started, Jim found me and stood next to me while I was worshipping Jesus during the worship music. He humbled himself and raised his hands like everyone else to get into worship. Suddenly, power entered him from his feet up to his head, which shocked him. He could feel the love of God entering him and filling his eyes with tears, but Jim fought back those tears, fearing what people would think of him. When he could not hold them in any longer, he starting weeping like a baby, just like all those at church whom he had mocked, thinking they were wimps.

Church was over and we came back home. As I walked in the door, I saw Jim on the couch, ready to share with me his experience at church. We had not communicated for the previous three weeks. He told me, “Today I experienced the power of God, and I realized that this is the love I was looking for! This love is better than sex! I don’t need you or anyone else.”

What I just heard him speak was a miracle! For someone like him to say that the love of God was better than sex was without a doubt a work of God. Suddenly he did not need sex or any person. Now it was going to be just Jim and Jesus spending time with each other and Jim learning about Him. This was like the experience I’d had with the Holy Spirit up at Big Bear. Jesus had touched my heart too and delivered me of the spirit of lust—of needing to have a man next to me.

God knows how to deliver us out of our weaknesses and heal our souls, with the strength to put aside the craving of unhealthy relations and more.

Our new journey began, and we started going to church every week to learn the Word of God. Pastor Henry's church was full of single people looking for mates, so it was important to prepare the congregation for godly marriage, since many of them were involved in lustful relationships. The pastor said, "I am conducting a three-month class entitled "Premarital Counseling for Those Who Are Thinking about Getting Married."

When I got home from church, I heard the voice of God speak to me, saying "I want you to ask Jim to go to counseling classes with you." I said, "What! We are no longer together, and I feel no love to marry him. Besides, he will not go because I asked him to do it a year ago." God replied, "Trust me. This is the man I have for you."

God is always right! Jim and I signed up for premarital counseling, which started two weeks later. My heart softened enough to open up to the possibility that we might get married.

Our first counseling session took place with Pastor Nona, Henry's wife. She had many questions, and some of them were hard to answer, like, How long have you been dating? Are you living together? What are your feelings about marriage? What came out of Jim's mouth was a list of "nevers."

Never wanted to get married; never wanted to have children; never wanted to be far from his parents, as they were number one; never liked pets; and never liked having anyone "too close to me."

Jim did not realize at the time that his life was about to make a 360-degree turnaround. My pastors had no hope for us and did not recommend marriage for us. But we stayed in the classes for three months like everyone else.

Surprise! Jim and Trish announced their wedding, to take place on December 11, 1988, in Las Vegas. We were the first couple to jump into a new commitment. There had been too many confirmations from God to ignore, and these confirmations gave us the strength to set aside everyone's opinions. Even our friends thought we were not a good match, but God's plan for us was a high calling, and a big price was already paid for it by Jesus.

Just a month before our wedding day, we were invited to the Coffee Roaster in Marina Del Rey by my friend Amy to hear a speaker by the name of Scott David. This coffee house was owned by a Christian man who would host fellowship with guest speakers sharing the Word of God (the Bible). It was a happening place, and many of the locals came to hear the speakers.

Scott David and his wife, Annette, were an amazing couple and very articulate about the Bible, sharing from the book of Revelation. This is one of the hardest books to understand because it describes the end times and what will happen in the future—that the earth will be destroyed, but a new earth and heaven will be created.

Jim's ears were very attentive to Scott's words, and he invited him to come to our apartment to share more about the subject. I agreed and I knew that God was going to use Scott and Annette in our lives in a very positive way, but they preferred to come share at our place *after* we got married.

On December 11, 1988, Jim and I were married in a simple wedding with the immediate family and two best friends. The ceremony was held in a Las Vegas chapel next to the Sahara Hotel.

Now the time came for us to host Scott and his wife, Annette, and I was feeling that I needed to invite others to my apartment as well. This was a perfect time to share Christianity with our family and close friends. They all needed Jesus! I had seven guests coming, and we were so excited.

Our guests and speakers arrived at our small two-bedroom apartment that had seven chairs and a couch in the living room. Scott opened in prayer, and his wife led us in singing a few Christian worship songs. The power of the Holy Spirit was present in the room, and I knew something special was happening in peoples' lives. It was a divine setup for God to empower Jim with a new heavenly language.

Remember, I mentioned about my miracle healing of my ears and how I also got my heavenly language—speaking in other tongues. Jim had never received this special gift, and he wanted it badly because he saw how powerful it was to use in daily life. Other ministers had prayed over him in the past, but it did not manifest at those times. Jim was feeling rejected by God, thinking that the gift of tongues was not for him.

Scott was praying for a friend of ours, and she had an amazing healing in her heart, as well as receiving the gift of her heavenly language. Jim watched this happen and was provoked to say, "I want that!"

Scott looked at Jim and asked, "Brother, have you received the gift of the Holy Spirit?" He said, "Yes, and I feel His presence." "Then humble yourself and receive the gift of the Holy Spirit." Suddenly the power of God took over Jim's mouth, and he began to speak in other tongues and with power! His face was radiant, and his eyes were angelic. He had received the best gift of his life, and from this point on, there was no turning back to the old lifestyle of the playboy.

Our life from that point forward went through dramatic changes, such as giving up smoking, drinking, and nightclubs, and disconnecting from party friends. "What in the world happened to Trish?" my friends and business associates asked. I did not give up my makeup business, and we did continue with Steele Productions, but not representing all the beautiful, sexy models anymore. Now we were determined to stay focused on our new calling with Jesus.

We continued having weekly Bible studies at our apartment, led by Scott and Annette David. Five months into it, many people were attending from all walks of life. Most of them were people from the entertainment industry, because when Jim and I would go on the studio sets, we would take our Bibles and invite people to come to our fellowship. Miracles were taking place, and people were getting healed, delivered from demons, delivered from drug and alcohol addictions, and healed from bone injuries.

There was another sudden change. Scott and Annette announced that they would be leaving for Europe to preach the Gospel. They wanted Jim to take over the Bible study, to teach, pray, and minister. Jim was shocked and responded, "No way! I am not equipped to do this." Scott said, "Jesus is going to train you; this is your new calling."

Jim was not equipped to teach anything. English was his second language, and he spoke in such broken English that it was difficult to get a full sentence out of him. He had taken a course at a community college in Glendale but did not learn to read and write English. Nevertheless, God the Holy Spirit taught him to read, write, and preach the Word. Jim fell in love with learning English through the stories of the Bible, which he read from beginning to end. He spent hours, days, and months studying the Bible during a period of disability due to a job accident.

What perfect timing for Jim to take time to learn and tend to the teaching by the Holy Spirit. I was so supportive of him learning to preach God's Word. It also helped to accelerate change in his personality, which had been one of arrogance, with a hot temper and narrow-mindedness; he had no trust in people. Thus, though our marriage had its rocky roads, by the grace of God, we drove right over them.

One afternoon, I was hosting a meeting at NBC Studios in Burbank. This was a new opportunity for me to network with those in the television industry and to share my gifts as a makeup/ hairstylist/wardrobe consultant for television.

I met a lovely lady named April Shenandoah, who was a dancer and actress. I invited her to my Bible study, and she came that week. She shared about arthritis in her hands that caused her pain; doctors had no cure for it. Jim said to her, “Let me pray that you be healed in the name of Jesus!” The miracle happened instantly; April was healed! She mentioned that she’d been to many healing services and the pain had never left, but that day it left! To this day, she is still healed and is greatly used of God across the country, sharing the Good News of Jesus, and she is also an author of three books. She was also a part of a prayer team at the White House in Washington. We are in touch, and she is a great inspiration to the body of Christ.

Another wonderful woman I want to mention is Iretha Bradford. She is a very educated, beautiful black lady with a doctor’s degree in education. She was married to a doctor in chemistry. She was a great influencer in teaching people how to have a relationship with the Holy Spirit and Jesus. We became her weekly attendees and her spiritual children, as she had no children of her own. Today she is ninety-four years old and still talking to people about Jesus.

My life was moving along with a whole new outlook, new friends, and new passions. Our weekly Bible studies were bringing people into our spiritual temple to inspire everyone in their giftings, like music and acting. Since we were near Hollywood and worked there, we found opportunities to share our belief in Jesus and to talk about Him.

As a leader in a group of talented Christians meeting monthly at NBC Television Studio for lunch, my husband and I came up with a great idea—"Concerts with a Vision"!

It was January of 1989, and we had an open invitation to attend a big gathering at a beautiful, huge church in Glendale, where we lived. A famous Christian evangelist was in town to share his message, along with a band that did great music. I was so inspired by the speaker and the Christian band. My love for music and performance was about to make a comeback.

April Shenandoah and Lu Lollio hosted the "Concerts with a Vision," and their team of talented people performed at the event. Jim Steele was the ending "act," sharing the Gospel of Christ and giving an altar call for people to come up for prayer. I was the producer and director running the show, which I love to do.

It had been two years since I had produced any productions, especially those in the nightclubs. My gifts had never left me, and now they were being used for Jesus!

Discover Trish's Mindset

WHAT HAPPENED TO HER MIND? SHE BECAME OPEN TO A SPIRITUAL MINDSET AND FOUND TRUTH AND FREEDOM! "YOU SHALL KNOW THE TRUTH, AND THE TRUTH SHALL MAKE YOU FREE." (JOHN 8:32)

Chapter 5

The '90s: Taking On The High Calling

As we moved into the '90s, things became much busier. We now started to expand our "Concerts with a Vision." Since so many people were now looking to attend, we had to move to a huge auditorium near the Los Angeles Zoo. It was a beautiful hall and just big enough for our needs.

A new development was having Richard and Bonita Zier produce the event. These two saw a greater vision for the concert, and they wanted to create a national magazine. Richard and Bonita had become great friends, and till this day, they have kept their course to spread the Gospel through music and a magazine called *Zoe International*.

As technology progressed, home videos and cable TV became more and more popular. The craze was all around us. The world was changing at such a rapid pace. This was called the "Z" generation, or Zoomers!

There were many opportunities around me, and so despite being very busy, I decided to take up a project. I knew I needed to spread a message to the women out there, especially those who felt helpless or were going through problems. They needed to hear the kind of message I had to share. I wanted to help them, to bring them closer to God, to heal them.

The project that I decided to take up was a television show. It consisted of recordings of testimonials of women and men whom God had helped, with the sharing of miracles and victories in their lives.

Multiple episodes of this were recorded, and it became quite popular, with a large viewership. *Women Crowned in Glory* and my husband's show, *True Life*, both gained a lot of traction and became renowned.

It was a huge effort, considering that we had to learn to direct, produce, write, and everything else on these TV shows. The success was pleasing to us, as it was the fruit of our hard work. Till this day, we see the impact of these shows. Just recently, one of our fans from the year 1997 left an inheritance for my charity.

My life following Jesus was amazing, with favorable surprises. I hope you are getting the picture of what it is like to serve God and follow His footsteps.

Also, during this time, Christian television was taking to the airwaves to get the news out to the world. Networks such as Trinity Broadcast Network (known as TBN) grew to be the largest Christian network in the world. The *700 Club*, hosted by Pat Robertson, was an amazing show that interviewed celebrities and notable people every week on channel 11, which is a secular station.

As I am writing this chapter, it brings back memories of the famous show called *The Joy Show*, hosted by Jay Jones on the TBN station. Jim and I were invited as guests on the show to share our testimony of how God saved and transformed our lives. Our story so touched Jay that he said, "You need to be a guest on another show called *Back on Course*, hosted by Gavin and Patti Macleod."

WOW! This was a divine setup from God, for we shared our story with Gavin Macleod, the boat caption of the television series called *The Love Boat.* That show was one of my favorite television series in the '80s. The four of us hit it off during the show, and they wanted to keep in touch with us, which they did.

Fast forward: after thirty years of friendship with the Macleod's, Jim and I have been conducting Bible studies in their home in Rancho Mirage, California, for the last five years. Gavin went to be with Jesus on May 29, 2021, and his wife, Patti, is still in touch. Have you ever wondered what these big television stars are like in person? Well, Gavin was a kind man, and nothing was fake about him. He also had a praying wife that transformed his life and caused him to be a wonderful husband and man of God.

Prayer works! It is the key to open God's heart to reach out to those whom you love and whose lives you want to see transformed. Remember in chapter 4, I prayed for God to save my playboy boyfriend, and look what happened—he became a saint!

Now back to my story, in which more people, changes, and stories made our life a major adventure. My husband came from a large family who were rather set in their ways. My in-laws had eight kids, including my husband, and they were firm believers in family values. My husband, the oldest son, had to carry on the family name, have a child, and be the leader of the younger siblings. For Jim, this was not what he had in mind for his life.

I already had a child from a previous marriage, whom Jim was content to raise as his own. Jim was the bachelor type. No marriage and no kids. So, when this sort of request came in from his parents, he found himself in conflict.

I was all for it. I did not mind having another child, even though I was ten years older than Jim and was warned by doctors about pregnancy and birthing at my age. Still, I was ready.

I knew what his parents truly desired: they wanted us to have our own child, which I understood and agreed with. It was confirmed by God to move forward—confirmed by the cost-free medical insurance that was given to me for anything related to the pregnancy.

The task of convincing Jim was surprisingly easy after I became pregnant. I thought it would be difficult for him to see me pregnant, but it wasn't. He was sweet, kind, and caring throughout my pregnancy. It seemed he was on board the whole time, even attending the classes with me.

The problem came later in my pregnancy when I heard the doctor's opinion about putting my body through the risk of having a child at the age of forty. But I knew God wanted me to have this child and that I was to pray over my pregnancy daily with my husband.

I also wanted to have this child the natural way, so Jim and I joined the Lamaze classes for childbirth. It teaches special breathing patterns and other natural relaxation techniques for dealing with pain. Jim was my amazing coach, who accompanied me through the dramatic birthing of a precious daughter. "Push, breathe, push again, breathe," he urged on and on until our girl arrived. My husband felt like he gave birth too! He had an awesome experience seeing our daughter emerge and felt the breath of God's Spirit in her.

My husband provided faith and support, which I would carry through to birthing many things throughout our lives together. I felt as if this mothering task was sent to me by God Himself and confirmed in a dream. In the dream, I saw myself in a hospital bed with my daughter in my arms and Jim standing there with another child in his arms.

I awakened from that dream claiming with certainty that we were having twins. So, when my darling Michelle was born in June of 1992, I was confused.

I asked God what He meant by twins. I got my answer when He came to me and told me that the vision meant something a little different than what I had interpreted.

My dream meant that I would have a child, and my husband would have a baby of his own, in the sense that he would finally birth his own church, a Foursquare Church.

In 1927, a denomination called the Foursquare Church was started by a woman called Aimee Semple McPherson. She became widely famous in the United States for helping World War I survivors and people suffering through the Great Depression, by feeding them and supplying aid for their emergency needs. Aimee was a trailblazing woman in Los Angeles who held unusual Pentecostal services at the Angeles Temple, which she had built to invite Hollywood and the local communities, filling thousands of seats.

In one very unforgettable service for the Hollywood community and the Los Angeles Police Department, she drove a big motorcycle onto the stage, jumped off it, and blew a whistle, saying, "Stop! You are all under arrest by the Holy Spirit."

Her brand of healing and faith drew so much attention that she had biographies written and documentaries filmed about her. She easily garnered nationwide attention in news and television, and she even had the first Christian float in the Rose Parade. These events filled my husband and me with the inspiration to bring the vision of his church to fruition. He was about to nourish a new congregation and take on many responsibilities. My husband was a Jordanian

American pastor. Along with him, a woman, Linda Oakland, was also heading her church, and right beside them, a Messianic Jew, Rabbi Murray, was helping his congregation. In Woodland Hills (in the San Fernando Valley), my husband and these two others rented a building. Congregations gathered for each service on Saturdays and on Sundays.

And so, the church, being our long-held dream, became the metaphorical child that I had seen my husband holding in the dream, bringing the dream to reality.

We had never expected to become pastors, but such was life and here we were. It was indeed a new time for us, and thank God for Don Long, supervisor of Foursquare Headquarters, and Linda Oakland, who saw the high calling in our life.

Using that facility was such a blessing for us. And our congregations blessed us too. Every church has a worship team, and we found a family who were all singers: the Veith Family—Johnny, Michaelina, and their three lovely daughters, all of whom had gifted voices.

This family came to us as Jim and I had our Bible studies as part of our weekly presentation. Someone had invited Johnny over; he asked if he could play our piano, and heavenly music began to flow like we'd never heard before. My piano had been sitting unused in my living room for years, and now it was being resurrected under the hands of this amazing pianist. Jim and I never played piano. Our piano was a gift to my daughter Shawna, but she stopped playing at a young age. After a few weeks, we found out that Johnny had separated from his wife and daughters, but prayers brought them back together the following month.

They needed a place for their family to stay for a month while they made the transition from Las Vegas to the San Fernando Valley. We therefore opened our two-bedroom apartment to the family of five to share the spare bedroom. We almost felt like missionaries. They were not the only guests to whom we offered our spare room over the years.

Life was moving in a new direction. I was getting to fulfill my dreams, all the while spreading the message of God. I could not have been happier. God was changing my husband into a godly minister and prophet.

Do you know what a prophet is? A person regarded as an inspired teacher or proclaimer of the will of God.

We were surrounded by many strong evangelists, prophets, and pastors, and we were learning all that God wanted to fulfill in our lives. As part of the Foursquare movement, we traveled to other states for annual conventions, meeting people from all over the world.

We kept in touch with Scott David (since the '80s), who was the Indiana Jones of the Gospel of Jesus. One day, Scott invited us to join him in a flight over the city of Hollywood to pray in the air. What in the world were we doing? We were praying against the Satanist churches that were planted throughout the city. We had with us the LaVey grandson, who'd escaped from his evil family, showing us where the churches were. Talk about an Indiana Jones experience. This was it! Evil still exists, but it is up to us to turn away from it and pray that the forces of evil go back to hell where they belong. Spirits are real, and though I'm not trying to scare you, I do want to enlighten you with insight of the real spiritual world that we do not see.

Some people have had their eyes opened to the spiritual realm that God Himself has created. "In the beginning God created the heavens and the earth. The earth was without form, and void; and darkness was on the face of the deep. And the Spirit of God was hovering over the face of the waters." This is mentioned in the first chapter of the Bible, so look it up. There is so much to share, but this chapter cannot contain it all.

Many other mighty men began to take on their high callings in life, and they were invincible. My husband was one of them, and when he prayed to God to raise up mighty men, several of them came across our path.

In 1990, Bill McCartney, a head football coach of the University of Colorado in Boulder, was called to start the Promise Keepers, a global evangelical Christian movement calling men back to being courageous and bold Christian leaders in their homes and businesses. Thousands of Promise Keepers showed up in front of the White House, repenting of their sins and turning back to their wives and families.

Wow! Life was amazing, seeing so many beautiful souls that loved God and were following their true calling to live the life of holiness, righteousness, love, kindness, patience, happiness, and much more. For it is all in Christ Jesus! Are you wondering if there is hope for you to have a new life? Jesus paid the price for the whole world, that you may have life and have it abundantly. God is good, and He wants everyone to come to His Son Jesus, who gave Himself on the cross and died. But He was raised the third day, resurrected to be with the Father, that you may also have eternal life.

This is very profound and may be hard to understand, for only the Holy Spirit can draw you to receive Jesus into your heart and be born again! Become a new person and live for an eternal purpose that is everlasting. Just say, "Yes! I want You, Jesus!" Watch what happens. You will begin to enjoy the goodness of God which you have not known. So many have said yes!

Have you ever wondered if there is such a thing as the perfect family or the perfect life? I thought there was no such thing because of all I had experienced in my early years. Life is a blessing and can be made perfect for those who seek to emulate the character of Jesus Christ. I met such a family—the William Hinn family. My husband and I were introduced to William Hinn, the brother of the big-time television evangelist, by one of our church members.

William Hinn is married to Theresa, who is a singer with the voice of an angel, and they bore four children. All their children are very close to each other, and today they are all married to godly mates that only God could have brought to them. They are loving, fun, talented, caring individuals that live the example of Jesus. Today my husband and William are the best of friends and minister to one another.

This is the beauty of the Kingdom of God and the saving grace of Jesus, that you can have wonderful people who really care about you and help you heal from all your past pain, sorrow, and mistakes.

There were more men that said “Yes! Take me and use me, Jesus!” Men like Tim Storey, the anointed evangelist that traveled to seventy-five countries and spoke to millions of people about the Gospel of Jesus. Today he is an acclaimed author, speaker, and life coach, known for inspiring and motivating people from all walks of life—including those in Hollywood, like Oprah Winfrey.

Timothy is a good name, meaning “one who honors God.” There was also Tim Perior, who had powerful spiritual gifts. His weekly Bible studies were packed with people, with many waiting outside of his small house. He was a very unusual writer and producer for God for many years, until he was taken home in 2019 in the glory of God.

And thirdly, Tim Davis. He started the Cleansing Stream at Church on the Way, which was pastored by Jack Hayford. Many marriages, people, and children were delivered from past trauma, demons, and pain in their bodies. After this man prayed for me, the spirits of shame, abuse, and all my past pain left my body, leaving me feeling free and clean—a new woman in just five minutes. Is there something you need prayer for to feel free from addictions, fears, shame, and any bondage? Jesus can do it through faith in Him as the great miracle Healer. Perhaps you need to call someone you know that is a strong Christian for prayer, for the miracle hotline works 24/7.

God used one particular woman to help me to understand how to live a life of service and pastoring. Beverly Bradford was the wife of a pastor at El Monte Foursquare Church and one of the most beautiful ladies I had ever known. I met her through some channels of friends, and she took me under her wing and helped me understand all there was about being a pastor's wife.

My ministry, Women Crowned in Glory, was taking off. We were getting attention and helping women who had been through or currently were in unfortunate domestic-abuse circumstances.

I was quite glad to learn from Beverly Bradford, because who was better to teach me and guide me than the wife of a pastor? Except a pastor, of course.

During that time, I met Reeni Fenholt, the wife of Jeff Fenholt, who was a famous rock-and-roll musician from the '60s that starred in the musical *Jesus Christ Superstar.* I mentioned him earlier. Reeni was an amazing woman of such grace and beauty that only God could groom her soul after all she went through in years of an abusive marriage to Jeff. We bonded closely, for it was divine for God to allow me to comfort her during her times of trouble. Today she is remarried to a wonderful godly man of great love and patience. I was there for her new wedding.

Jim and I got to know all these people I have mentioned quite well. It was an eye-opening experience, I must say. I was immersed and taking things at my own pace, and I kept learning from these godly families, evangelists, and pastors' wives.

Miracles do happen, and I, of course, do believe in them. I have seen so many of them happen in seconds. Miracles come out of nowhere and demonstrate God's grace.

My husband and I had a divine appointment with another minister who works in the gift of miracles, Mr. Eric Holzaphel and his lovely wife, Angelika. They came to us to have my husband take photographs of Angelika for her passport. She was originally from Germany.

My husband was a great photographer when I met him, and he was still in demand for his great photos up till the year 2000. Photography was Jim's fun hobby while working a full-time job with Wanamaker Rentals in the '80s. The story about his gift with photography will have to be told in another book, but suffice it to say that his worked blessed many people and divinely connected souls together.

Angelika ended up with excellent photos for her passport. She and Eric were introduced to the Foursquare denomination through us, and today they travel around the Asian countries conducting miracles services. We have stayed friends till this day, and Angelika has been active on my Advisory Board for over twenty years.

In 1994, the earthquake hit L.A. County—more specifically, Northridge. It was one of the worst earthquakes the U.S. had ever seen, economically speaking: magnitude 6.7 on the Richter scale. Thousands of people were displaced. It was a mess.

We were living in the Northridge area at the time the earthquake hit. It was a harrowing experience, as my husband and I took our baby, Michelle, and ran out onto the street. The shaking of the ground and the sheer power of the earthquake were terrifying. My heart skipped several beats, I'm sure.

We came out onto the street and saw many other people also terrified. Some had never experienced an earthquake before and were even more terrified than us. Even the aftershocks were nerve-racking.

As the earthquake subsided, we saw everyone holding each other and just praying, praying to God. Praying to whatever deity they believed in. Even those who weren't too inclined to have faith were looking toward a higher power in that frightening moment. It warmed my heart to see that, ultimately, people would always come back to God and see that it was a miracle, *His* miracle, that we all survived and lived to see another day. His grace was immense.

My husband's church and ministry helped those who had lost someone or were displaced. We took them in and gave them shelter, food, and hope. We just wanted to help them.

Tragedies are inevitable. They happen at the strangest of times. They happen no matter if you try to prevent them or not.

In the Middle East, there is a tradition of arranged marriages. Parents set up their daughters to marry men they think would be good for the family, but they don't necessarily get to know who those men really are. Well, my husband's oldest sister had a bad experience with an arranged marriage.

My ministry is all about helping women out of abusive relationships and situations, to nurture and rebuild them. So, when we heard that Jim's sister, Jahad, was not happy with and felt stuck in her arranged marriage, we wanted to help her.

What we didn't know was that this was an abusive relationship.

Jahad was living far from us, so we brought her out to stay with us, which was a massive relief to her. It seemed like the weight of the world had been taken off her shoulders.

She began to really enjoy herself, and we were glad that we were able to help someone escape a bad situation. My husband was relieved to see that after months of staying out here in California, his sister was happy and free from the pain of twelve years of abuse. My sister-in-law experienced a transformation at Bible study one evening, and she was the happiest I had ever seen her.

One morning after leaving Jahad at the pool with my daughter, who had taken quickly to her auntie, I went to a girlfriend's baby shower. Jim was at the house enjoying a day off.

All was well. But things have a way of taking a turn for the worse when you're not looking.

Michelle was only four years old around that time, so her walking from the pool to the front door of the house by herself was quite a feat. She banged on the door with her tiny hands until Jim opened the door. He wondered how she had gotten all this way without his sister. He looked for Jahad but didn't find her. He thought maybe she had dropped Michelle off and left.

He had the shock of a lifetime when he opened the door a little while later and found an officer standing there with a sad look on his face.

The officer described a woman to Jim, and Jim, of course, said, "That sounds like my sister," at which point the grim look on the officer's face became grimmer. The officer took him to the pool, and there was Jahad, face down, dead. She had drowned.

If there is anything a person is supposed to do in those circumstances other than cry over the body of their loved one, I don't know it yet. Because that is what Jim did—he sobbed and begged for her to come back to life. He was heartbroken and shattered. I didn't find out what had happened until I came back and asked people where he was.

When I saw him in that state, I was heartbroken too for her and for my husband. She was such a ray of sunshine, and then she was gone, just like that.

I comforted my husband because that was all I could do, really. We had our expectations, but God had other plans. I didn't know what God's plans were at first. But flashes came to me, and slowly those flashes became something more—a clearer picture: I saw a gorgeous place with green meadows and rivers flowing, gleaming like liquid moonlight. Birds chirping, flowers blooming. It felt like heaven. And *she* was there, laughing, frolicking, happy, and free. She was looking up at Jesus and saying, "Thank You so much for bringing me here!"

Seeing Jahad so beautifully happy was my realization that she had gotten to the best place in her life, where there is no fear or sorrow to be felt. I told Jim that she was free now and so happy to be there with Jesus. It was the most beautiful vision I had ever seen of heaven.

It was time for Jim to share with his parents that their daughter was dead. For the Haddads, it was a big loss. Jahad had been taken to America from Jordan at the age of eighteen. She never wanted to marry her husband, and now her life was gone.

A funeral was arranged that week, and hundreds of family members gathered for the burial. After the burial, there was a private gathering at the home of Mr. and Mrs. Haddad. A divine miracle was about to take place. As the men were outside sitting and waiting for the food to arrive, Jim's father, Aref, was talking to the priest that conducted the service and came to the house to bless the food. Aref mentioned to the priest that one of his sons was a pastor. The priest asked, "Where is he?"

"Come here!" Aref shouted to Jim, who was sitting a good distance away. Jim replied, "No, leave me alone." But Aref repeated, "Come now!" In respect to his dad, Jim walked over and was introduced to the priest.

The priest asked, "My son, where do you pastor?" "I pastor a Foursquare Church in Studio City. And do you know Pastor Jack Hayford, who is my supervisor of the churches?" "Yes, Pastor Hayford," the priest replied.

Suddenly the priest fainted into Jim's arms with his head on Jim's chest and began to weep like a baby. Jim was caught by surprise and held the priest with compassion. He began to pray for this man, hoping to comfort him but not realizing that the Holy Spirit was healing this man. Jim asked, "Father, are you okay?"

The priest shared with Jim that he had been sick at the hospital the day before with diabetes and prayed for God to heal him, "and now God is healing me at your hands!"

The priest raised up and with boldness said to Jim's father, "You invited me here to speak a blessing over the food and the house, but I came here to get a blessing from your son, Jim Steele. Listen to Jim, for he is one of Jesus's disciples." For years, all of Jim's family thought Jim had gone crazy when he became a born-again Christian. They used to mock Jim for his faith in Jesus, but now the priest, whom they all respected, was saying Jim was of God—he was not crazy or some religious freak! The movement of the Spirit was opening the stubborn hearts, and these men came to repentance and began respecting Jim for his high calling,

As for the priest, he became a new person by a miracle of God, and for ten years thereafter, people came to him for healing prayer after church. His was a Greek Orthodox church in Studio City. Revival took place there, and lives were changed.

My husband's prayer over his sister, Jahad, came to pass: "Father, credit her death for Your glory, for she did not live long enough." God did many miraculous things for the Haddads to assure them that Jahad was at peace.

The '90s for me and my family were a journey of exploring the world's gifted churches, ministers, and women that all loved God. Out of my women's ministry came my first book, entitled *Women Crowned in Glory: The Compelling Life-Changing Stories of 12 Women.*

Mr. Alex Clark, another amazing evangelist, gave me the funds to self-publish that book. It was written in less than a year, with twelve different women who tell their life stories about how they came to Christ. All these women were a part of my ministry as members or guest speakers. It was an international book of testimonies from Sweden, South Africa, Lebanon, Italy, and Germany. I never dreamed that I would write a book, but my own life story was included as one chapter. Writing was something I was not good at in school because of my hearing loss and lack of comprehension. I got the best writer to help me, and she is Nancy Baker, the first Christian lady I met, who hired me for the Jack LaLanne Health Spa. God brought her back into my life for a season for us to help each other grow in the new lives ahead of us. Nancy had been burnt out from trying to save her marriage, children, and businesses. Sometimes we must just let go and let God take the cares.

As you all know by now, my journey for the past forty years has been surrounded by music and fashion. In this chapter, I did not share who the popular artists were and what the fashion was like, but I was dancing in the spirit with the best gospel songs by the best artists and wearing heavenly fashions of white chiffon on stage.

Did you know that many of the greatest recording artists grew up singing in church first? Yes, people like Whitney Houston, Aretha Franklin, Elvis Presley, Jessica Simpson, Justin Bieber, and many more! But one of my favorite experiences in the '90s was with Smokey Robinson and Ivory Stone. Ivory Stone, a singer/songwriter, author, and minister, had introduced my husband and me to Smokey. Ivory was attending our church, and we prayed for God to open Smokey's home to start a fellowship, which he did, inviting people from Motown. Many in the industry attended, but the big highlight was Berry Gordy himself. Smokey was gracious, beautiful, and kind to share his life testimony and to give us a platform to win souls. Ivory was amazing with her beautiful spirit, making people feel comfortable in accepting the Spirit of God into their hearts.

Smokey Robinson and the Miracles were the greatest of their times, and the greatest miracle was Smokey. He was delivered from drug additions and more. Leon Isaac Kennedy, his best friend, was responsible for the great transformation in Smokey's life.

I remember many more who have come so far in their faith with God, for example, two who went "Up, Up, and Away in My Beautiful Balloon." Marilyn McCoo and Billy Davis, Jr. of the Fifth Dimension are God's generals that give the love of Christ and new sounds from heaven. We had the pleasure to be under their anointing of praise and music. Married for fifty years, they are still "Just Like Starting Over." They are full of spark!

Looking unto Jesus, the Author and Finisher of our faith! There is liberty in the Spirit of the Lord.

Discover Trish's Mindset

AS I ACCEPTED THE CALLING IN MY LIFE BY GOD, I KNEW I HAD TO CHANGE MY MINDSET AND LIFESTYLE TO RECEIVE THE BLESSINGS OF LIFE.

I "BESEECH YOU TO WALK WORTHY OF THE CALLING WITH WHICH YOU WERE CALLED, WITH ALL LOWLINESS AND GENTLENESS, WITH LONGSUFFERING, BEARING WITH ONE ANOTHER IN LOVE, ENDEAVORING TO KEEP THE UNITY OF THE SPIRIT IN THE BOND OF PEACE." (EPHESIANS 4:1-3)

Chapter 6

The 2000s: Y2k—A New Era

I've seen a lot of change throughout my life. The many eras, the shifting technologies and social conventions. But the turn of the millennium must have been the sharpest change I'd ever seen the world face. Things changed so quickly; it was as if the world was in a race.

But what was it racing against? No one could tell. Y2K was big. Many of the readers might remember Y2K and how crazy it was. There was widespread fear of major systems and stock markets crashing because the digital clocks on their computers wouldn't turn from 1999 to 2000. As a result, the world economy would crash, the nukes would be released, and an apocalypse would be unleashed on the earth. At least, that is what some crackpot conspiracy theorists thought. But in the end, nothing happened that they had prophesied. The clocks turned from 1999 to 2000. The new millennium arrived, and those who had prepared fallout shelters looked embarrassed by the end.

The new millennium brought with it new ideas, new visions, and new ways to further progress our work of spreading the Word of God and helping women.

Things changed drastically when Joy Zachariou declared that God was calling me to take Women Crowned in Glory to all of Southern California. She and her husband, Panos, were very inspirational and talented. They had two sons, and the whole family were gospel singers around the world. Jim and I had known them for three years, and they'd performed at our church many times.

Joy worked at the State Capitol in Sacramento for many years and told me about her experiences helping non-profit organizations. She felt the same Spirit of God that I felt. I felt like I could relate to her and learn from such a godly beautiful woman, wife, and mother of two amazing boys.

I told Joy about my work with Women Crowned in Glory. She was very impressed. By the turn of the millennium, I had already published my book by that name. She told me that she envisioned me starting my own non-profit.

That interested me, considering I wanted to further expand my work to help women who had been abused or were in an otherwise toxic environment, but I didn't really know how to do any of that. Apprehension took hold of me.

One night, God spoke to my heart and told me to follow the path Joy spoke of. He reminded me how I'd won all those pageants. I thought about it and realized it was my discipline and courage that had carried me through all that. God told me that the same discipline and courage would be required to make this thing a reality so that I could help more women. This was what I was meant to do. I made my decision.

With her joyous spirit, Joy Zachariou took the time to file my non-profit and bring the vision and mission of Women Crowned in Glory to the world.

By this time, my daughter Shawna was in her mid-twenties. She was well established, having graduated with her BA in Business from the University of Redlands and having worked for a corporation as a sales manager. She had taken a very different path from the one I had taken in my youth. I guess you could say that it was the new era. Or maybe it was how she was raised; she had become quite career oriented and sharp. That had also led to a slight distance between us that always seemed to be there. So, when I went to ask her for some money to get this non-profit registered, it was a little awkward.

But I was determined to bridge the gap. I told her about what I intended to do and the kind of money I needed. She had her own apprehensions, but when she realized how determined I was and how much I believed in the project I was about to undertake, she gave me the money. After I launched the project, she even joined me in helping the management side of things. I was reminded of how blessed I was.

The 2000s were a transitional time for my husband too. Through mutual decision, Jim decided to close the church. Though he was more passionate about ministry, he took a job at Macy's Department Store as a vendor for Chanel in order to invest in and support this venture of mine. But he could not help but preach the Good News in the marketplace. During the years he worked in the store's main-floor fragrance department, he ran a secret church in the stockroom, which for years brought people salvation and miracles. It's a wonder this was never revealed.

I highly recommend that you listen to the real miraculous stories of my husband's ministry at Macy's by attending one of his weekly Zoom meetings that he conducts today. He was an undercover agent for the Gospel of Jesus. Hundreds of people were touched and experienced the power of God!

Today, my non-profit is known as Safe Passage Heals. After several board meetings with my staff, Pat Storey, Bonnie Corwin, and the board of directors, we came up with the name, which fit perfectly as a DBA. Names are very important to reach out to the community and to apply for grants. We have helped women who were in bad situations and wanted to leave those abusive traps. We have given a "safe passage" to them.

Unfortunately, the name "Women Crowned in Glory" didn't really catch on, but instead it became the umbrella name of the non-profit. My background experience in pageants, makeup, and beauty care was embedded in the program I created called "Stepping Stones to a New Life," to win the crown of glory of God's plan for these abused women.

Safe Passage took off greater than ever just by my being *fearless* in sharing my testimony to the different shelters and other charities. Now I clearly understood the ministry of Jesus, for He Himself went out to share the Good News of salvation, mostly in the marketplace, where thousands came to believe and followed Him. That same anointing was on me as I shared what Jesus did for me and how His love was unchangeable.

I get so excited when I think about it right now! I want to give *you* a safe passage to a new life. Are you ready to receive it? If so, say this prayer: "Jesus, come into my life. Forgive me of my sins. I believe You are the Son of God, and You died for me to have eternal life. Fill me with Your Spirit, that I may be born again. Thank You, Jesus, Amen."

If you prayed this prayer, you have become born again and the Holy Spirit will come to you to bear witness that Jesus is alive and knows you by name. Just find a Christian church nearby and get a Bible so you may understand the will of God for your life.

There is so much to learn about the dignity of Jesus and His character, power, and love. I want the Holy Spirit to teach you all that I have learned from the good, the bad, and the ugly.

On September 11, 2001, the World Trade Center was hit. As many as 2,977 people died, and over 25,000 were injured, with substantial long-term health consequences, in addition to a least $10 billion in infrastructure and property damage.

It remains the deadliest disaster in the history of the U.S. Do you remember it?

Recently, former President George W. Bush called on Americans on Saturday, September 11, 2021, to confront domestic violent extremists, comparing them to violent extremists abroad and warning that they are "children of the same foul spirit."

In a speech marking the twentieth anniversary of the 9/11 attack, Bush said the U.S. has seen "growing evidence that the dangers to our country can come not only across borders, but from violence that gathers within."

Some people may be wondering, "Where was God during this time?" He was there, seeing it all, and those who chose to do evil could not be controlled, for God gives us all a choice to live a life of peace or evil. Our job is to pray for the protection of our country, families, and loved ones. We cannot live in fear but live in divine oneness with the heavenly Father, who can give us peace.

Around this same time, my supporters and friends of Safe Passage gathered to help send relief to the families that were affected by this attack. It was a violent act of murder, and domestic violence is the same type of act. There have been many deaths at the hands of partners whom the victims loved.

I am always praying for our country and for violence to stop, and that Jesus will come soon to deal with all the evil that is going on today.

God has protected me from many dangerous situations just because I or someone was praying for my life. Is there someone you know who is in danger or hurting from illness that needs a miracle? Pray! Jesus is the same yesterday, today, and forever, and He hears all prayers.

Now, I would like to get back to my story and share more of my *divinely connected* life. By this time, I had just turned fifty, the golden jubilee year!

Fifty is no longer what it uses to be. Some cultures believe that reaching age fifty is the golden age that deserves special, respectful attention. Well, that is exactly what was taking place in this new era of the decade 2000 to 2010.

My mindset was focused on the accomplishments of half a century of my life, making the world brighter! I was transforming others' lives to be fierce, fabulous, and focused, to win back their identities.

By this time, we were living in Van Nuys, and our daughter Michelle was seven years old. She had seen the series of movies called *The Lion King* 1, 2 and 3—great, compassionate stories my husband and I also loved. Michelle took on the character of Simba and started jumping onto her father's lap to get his attention when she wanted something. And she used that character to her advantage.

Remember Jim had a list of "nevers," and one was never to have pets! Well, Daddy gave Michelle her first pet. We had to start small, with a bird. So, we got her two budgerigars, also known as the common parakeet. One was blue and the other was green. Michelle named them after her favorite Bible characters—the male was named David and the female was named Mary.

Never say “never.” You might rob yourself of a blessing that can change your life and bring forth joy.

Next were two small dogs that one of the members of our church had to give away because she was moving. The male was named Charlie, and the female was Gismo. They were small Shih Tzus. Michelle started dressing them up as dolls, and from that point on, her creativity began to blossom. She must have spent hours talking to her dogs about her designs to make them look fashionable.

But that was not the end of having pets. After giving back the dogs to the original owners, we found a small visitor at our doorstep. Guess who’s coming to dinner? Kitty Mat.

God led this small lost kitten to our doorstep to be fed and adopted. This cat became the best pet we ever had. He was like the cartoon character Garfield. Michelle named him Kitty Mat, and he became the king of the neighborhood cats.

Today, cats and dogs are used as service animals to give comfort, healing, and love to people who have gone through traumas in their lives. We all need someone or something to help us heal from our past pain. Do you need a Safe Passage or a safe animal?

Back to my charity: it was at this time that we were producing three events a year to raise funds for the Safe

Passage Home and its program, "Stepping Stones to a New Life" for abused women to heal and become self-sufficient.

Many celebrities and VIPs attended our events, like Gary Marshall, Taylor Armstrong and Beverly Hills Housewives, Lee Benton, Hunter Tylo, Chuck Woolery and Susan Stafford, Stella Stevens, Brenda Epperson, Jennifer O'Neil, Smokey Robinson, Leon Patillo, Pat and Debby Boone, Alfie Durio, Jackie Kallen, Giuseppe Franco, Kim Vo, and famous realtor Elaine Young, some of whom made time to serve as board members of my charity.

A divine connection that only God could make by His Holy Spirit was for me to meet Beverly Cohen, the owner of the Four Seasons Hotel in Beverly Hills, and the one-and-only Jeannie Jones, the artist for Smash Box cosmetics.

Our first Safe Passage gala was held at the Four Seasons in Beverly Hills, with a fashion show conducted by actress Hunter Tylo and her celebrity friends, featuring phenomenal Jeannie Jones handbag and accessories fashions. The luncheon was packed out with live entertainment and a silent and live auction, with the Steven La Vaggi Awards given out to two special people: Elaine Young and Rebecca Pollock (an overcomer of domestic violence).

Jeannie Jones and I became the event producers for the next five years. Today, she is my image stylist and true sister in Christ. There were people there that I had never met but who embraced the charity with all their hearts, supporting the cause for many years. But one lady who wanted to know my husband and me deeply was Beverly Cohen. She came up and introduced herself to us. The next thing we knew, my husband was invited to go with Beverly in a limousine to Cedar Sinai Hospital to pray for her brother-in-law. I had to stay to close the event. Beverly knew that my husband was a Christian minister.

My husband had studied the Jewish traditions and the Hebrew Bible, which the Jews call the Tanakh, for years, so he felt very comfortable praying over her brother-in-law. The grace of God was there, and my husband prayed in Jesus's name. He got better and left a few days after the prayer. Beverly had also agreed in prayer with my husband, and she felt the power of the Holy Spirit all over her.

Today, twenty years later, we are still friends, and she supports my charity as well as her charity and many others. She is a blessing to the community!

There are hundreds of charity events that take place every month in Los Angeles County, which shows the great need in our communities. I had the pleasure to help Agnes Nicole Winter, a Beverly Hills realtor and Swedish actress who started her own charity called C.A.P. (Children's After-School Programs). It was a success, helped along by her two sons, Cristofer and Alex.

I want to thank all the people that attended my charity events to support the mission of saving and transforming lives over the years. You know who you are, and forgive me if your name is not in this story, for my mind of Steele may be strong but sometimes weak in remembering people's names. I would love to reconnect with the thousands of people I have met over the past thirty years in the non-profit world, from True Life Church to Safe Passage Heals. *You are all special* to me! Just like my grandmother said, "*You are special.*" It takes one special person to meet another special person and keep the goodness of their hearts flowing.

Several events took place in Beverly Hills over the years 2000– 2018 but also in the San Fernando Valley, which is where our office is located and where my family lived for thirty years.

I have wonderful memories of the events for Safe Passage at the CBS Radford Studios in Studio City, run by Michael Klausman, an amazing Christian who loved supporting charities that transformed people's lives. Michael also encouraged us to participate in the Studio City Christmas Parade in 2000. I designed two themes—one was Mary and Joseph in the stable with baby Jesus, the Christmas birth. We had our church members participate, and we included animals. This was sponsored by my husband's ministry, True Life Church.

And riding in a white convertible car for Safe Passage Heavenly Home were beautiful board members and my daughter Michelle, all wearing white angel wings and gowns, to express the love and safety of the charity.

Toluca Lake was another highlight at Cinema Secrets, owned by the famous makeup artist/educator for television and film, Mr. Maurice Stein, and his son Danny Stein. I can't thank them enough for all the pro-bono services they gave my women to look and feel beautiful again. Sherman Oaks was another destination and another divine connection. Mr. Eli Dafesh, the top entrepreneur for Kangen Water, was sent to our home to share about this water purification system. This water conversation turned into a testimony shared by my husband Jim about how he became a minister. Suddenly Eli realized he was meeting his cousin for the first time.

The Haddads were such a large group that many had never met face to face, even among the 400–500 guests at annual weddings we attended.

Eli and his wife, Jillina, became a new addition to the Safe Passage family and served on the board for many years. God has been gathering our new family in Christ before our eternal destiny.

There were also television appearances on *The Doctors* show. Dr. Andrew Orden, who donated services, attended to one of my ladies who was scarred badly from physical abuse.

For ten years, many dentists and doctors contributed their services: Dr. Peter Cheski, Dr. Faddad, Dr. John Vartanian, Dr. Bruce Vafa, Dr. Gould, and Dr. Bill Dorfman.

This charity was paying it forward! I was living out my words from the amazing doctor who spared me from the split forehead caused by an abuser in 1985. The ER doctor compassionately gave me a new forehead and left me scarless, with no payment due! Do you remember reading this in chapter 4?

At that time, I said, *"One day I am going to pay it forward to help other women heal from domestic violence."* This was my first declaration to me and God. WOW!

My testimony and compassion opened many doors to doctors, dentists, fashion designers, makeup artists, and hair stylists. They were the "Extreme Makeover" team. These Safe Passage makeovers and stories were better than the television show itself that aired for five years.

And not to forget *Dancing with the Stars*, an evening that was so special to me, as dancing was my first love as a child. Thanks to Tina Malave, who introduced me to all the judges, dance instructors, and the stars and shared her passion about Safe Passage.

This was one of the highlights of my charity, fulfilling every desire to heal the souls of those who have been abused, through dancing and the joyful excitement of movement.

Today, Safe Passage has created a new project called "Healing through Movements," which is helping people to go outside, break away from fear, and get healthy through exercising, Zumba classes, self-defense, dancing, and more, to spring up joy in the body. *It helps keep you ageless!*

The years 2000 to 2010 brought about a new era for Safe Passage and my husband's ministry. We were the rich and famous (mindset) of the undercover Evangelists to save, heal, and impart the joy of Christ. Many heard our personal story, and many experienced Jesus Christ. I want to thank everyone who opened their homes for fellowship, allowing my husband to share the Good News of salvation. People like Susan Stafford, Patricia and Bob Correy, Elaine Young, Dr. Maria Simms, and Rosemarie Stein. It was like the Beverly Hills fever, with a hot message out of the mouth of a prophet to turn God's people back to Him.

Are you seeing the picture of the Mind of Steele? I was being all to all men and women that I may win them over to Jesus—the One who created them and died for them so they may have eternal life. This lifestyle has kept me *steadfast, fearless, and divinely connected.* Sharing God's love fuels me.

Take a moment and think about your life. Is it happy, fulfilling, and balanced? Can you say that you have done it all to reach the destiny of eternal life? Is anything missing? There is a heaven and a hell, and we have a choice to live in either one of these eternal environments. I am here to help guide you, so hold this thought until the end of my story.

Discover the Mind of God

"BLESS THE LORD, O MY SOUL, AND FORGET NOT ALL HIS BENEFITS: WHO FORGIVES ALL YOUR INIQUITIES, WHO HEALS ALL YOUR DISEASES, WHO REDEEMS YOUR LIFE FROM DESTRUCTION, WHO CROWNS YOU WITH LOVINGKINDNESS AND TENDER MERCIES, WHO SATISFIES YOUR MOUTH WITH GOOD THINGS, SO THAT YOUR YOUTH IS RENEWED LIKE THE EAGLE'S."
(PSALM 103:2-5)

Women Crowned in Glory

A SAFE PASSAGE

You shall also be a crown of glory in the hand of the L*ORD,*
and a royal diadem in the hand of your God. (Isaiah 62:3)

Chapter 7

The 2010s: An Unexpected Calling

The 2010s decade. What an exciting time. The age of fast information and social media. I'd seen the world change fast throughout my life, but the immense transformation the world went through in this decade was nothing like I'd ever seen before. Now, social media reigned supreme. The world was more connected than ever before. Technological advances were accelerated tenfold.

There used to be a time when the world slept. Now, though, it feels like the world is awake all the time. Unblinking.

Adapting to this new decade at my age was a new experience. Barack Obama was our president going into this new decade. An African American man was president for the first time in this country's history, and he stayed that way till 2016. What a monumental step.

The 2010s decade was the beginning of the movement era too. Everyone had a cause to fight for. Everyone had a voice they wanted to raise. Rightfully so. Everyone should have something to fight for. With the appointment and work of Barack Obama, a lot of wounds that had been open for a long time came to light. People started to raise awareness, and that began a chain reaction. Any group that felt marginalized or unfairly treated came forward to demand equal rights or acceptance. A lot of things started to become normalized.

I had a movement too. A cause that I was fighting for. The Jesus Movement—and I was so happy to be a part of it. Life was good. I still had my ministry, I had Safe Passage, I had my daughters, I had my husband, I had everything. I could not have asked for more—except being able to help more people, more women.

We'd been looking to move into the Woodland Hills area for some time. By divine setup, I met Mr. Mahdavi and his wife Nadya, and we discussed renting one of their properties. This family leased their home to us on Queen Victoria Road in a very private neighborhood, a beautiful area with gorgeous custom-made homes. It was one of their best properties, and it was not up for lease, yet they made it available to us. I thought that was very considerate. We soon became quite close to the couple. They helped us out a lot. In fact, they even started supporting my charity quite well too.

Speaking of charity events, that house in that area became the main hosting site for the charity events for Safe Passage and for my husband's ministry. The house was seated on two acres of land, with a pool and large patio areas to host hundreds of people comfortably.

It was also the location of the launch party for my daughter's newest clothing line, called "Cover Me Wear," a line of modest clothing. Michelle had transformed a room in the back of the house into a sewing/production room. And, of course, her mother was the manager of the whole thing.

I couldn't believe it at first, to be honest—here I was in my late fifties, and I was living my teenage dream of being a fashion designer. It took a long time—and somewhere along the line, I had gone into the makeup-industry side of things—but now I was finally getting to live my fashion-designing dreams, conceptualizing and applying all those ideas in my head.

And the fact that I was collaborating with my daughter was just the cherry on top. A true mother-daughter production. She was the creative one—she brought to the table all the new patterns, fabrics, and trends, and I just helped her fit the puzzle together.

The turnout for Michelle's launch party was pretty huge. We called all our friends who were models or could model. So many people, including celebrities, attended. The swimming pool in the backyard was the perfect place for a photo shoot featuring the line of clothing my daughter was producing. The bridge in the backyard was turned into a modeling runway/ramp.

To help us out, our dear friend Rosemarie Stein from Germany came. She was an immense presence, and her impeccable fashion sense helped us make the launch party a huge success. In fact, Rosemarie was always enormously helpful during all the time I knew her. She went to heaven and joined Jesus last year, and we miss her and remember her fondly.

One of the hardest things to do is to move. Due to some problems, our landlords asked for their house back. We had to find a new house by the end of the thirty-day notice. It became ever so difficult to find something in the same area, since Michelle was still in high school, and her school was within walking distance.

With the moving deadline approaching, we had to find a house fast, and we'd had no luck. I am sure you know the stress caused by having to find a place to live and then moving everything. But God sent me a beautiful rainbow over the Queen Victoria house to assure me that I would find the perfect place.

One day, my daughter Michelle and I drove past a beautiful house. The neighborhood was called Reseda, and it was around eight miles away from the Woodland Hills area. While the Woodland Hills area was decidedly affluent, this area wasn't.

So, my daughter and I decided to get out of the car to see if the gate was open so we could look at the house. The place was locked, and it seemed no one was home. Just as we turned to leave, disheartened, we saw a man pull up to the gate. He was the landlord! What a brilliant coincidence and a relief too. I asked him all the usual questions about the house, and he agreed to lease the house to us. He said he felt a divine presence in us.

When it came to moving day, we reached the house and saw him still cleaning up and tidying the place to get it ready for us to move in. The U-Haul truck came, and several friends from my husband's ministry started moving in our furniture. We had noticed that the landlord was still there finishing the cleaning, and he looked totally exhausted, with bloodshot eyes. Jim approached him, asking, "Are you feeling okay?" As the landlord shared his health issues, we knew it was time to pray and believe God for a miracle. We closed our eyes and asked God to heal him.

We opened our eyes, and his eyes weren't bloodshot anymore. In fact, he said he felt better than he had in years. I knew in that moment that I had just seen a miracle happen in front of me. And so did the man. He was so overjoyed and surprised. And he later understood that Jesus is a miracle worker. That rainbow I had seen, two days before moving, was God's promise to me that he had a new landlord and a new purpose for my family.

We lived there for the next nine years. I found an amazing office just a few miles from that house. A new location for the charity and for our family became the next big move of God to use us in the community.

There is so much to share that happened in my journey from 2010 to 2020, another decade with many unusual experiences that kept me *ageless, fearless, and divinely connected.*

Safe Passage Charity was the force that kept me moving, thinking, serving, giving, and loving others, because it was my passion. It was its own movement. Many people became advocates and a voice against domestic violence. I had as many as eighteen board members and thousands of supporters over the years. You'd think this would tire me out, but instead it kept me in shape. It's called exercising the mind, body, and spirit.

We had a public-service announcement on CBS/KCAL television airing weekly. We served hundreds of women and their children, earning a 95 percent success rate for breaking the cycle of abuse. I was the trailblazer with fifty years' experience in this field. No wonder many doctors, dentists, artists, and fashion designers all started taking time to pay it forward—I was a walking testimony of how women can be restored with a new life.

The statistics of domestic violence in Los Angeles were growing, and there was a big need for more charities like mine to open and help these people. It was time for me to begin to embrace a younger generation to carry on the vision of Safe Passage Heals.

On August 15, 2014, a very special lady came to my office with her PR person to discuss doing an event together. Her name was Luisa Diaz. She was a former Miss Venezuela International, and she had a flamboyant accent. I thought to myself that she might be an answer to one my prayers.

"Darling, I want to do an event for your charity because I have compassion on those who have been abused." Miss Diaz began to share more about her childhood and life in Venezuela. It was so amazing hearing the story of her beloved grandmother, a victim of domestic violence. This was not just some ordinary story of abuse. This woman was from a Latin culture, and she had escaped with her fifteen children and one granddaughter, Luisa, with her.

WOW—the story was deep, strong, and victorious! Luisa was taking on a new project on behalf of her brave and strong grandmother, creating a message of kindness to bring healing in the Latin community and the world.[1]

I felt her passion, and she felt my passion, and we embraced each other's visions. "Mi Amor Gala, a Celebration of Kindness," she called it. "Let get started planning now, for the event will take place in two months."

Now, that's what I call acting for the big attraction! Luisa put her heart and soul into the production and gathered the women around her that looked angelic. I was seeing myself in this woman twenty years younger than me, who had the same energy, compassion, and experience as I had and was able to make things flourish.

It was about time I found a passionate young lady with the same mindset and the same ethic background (I am a Blanco but raised as Middle Eastern) to embrace Safe Passage as her own. Luisa became my spiritual daughter and is still so to this day. So many wonderful things have happened between us and our passion to help others.

Since then, one of my beloved board members, Janet Cano, who has been with me for over ten years, has also

[1] You can check out Luisa's website at luisadiaz.com.

become a spiritual daughter. I have been her mentor over the years, teaching her the non-profit world in between her busy life as a wife, mother, and entrepreneur. Her daughter, Madalyn Cano, is my youngest advocate and has been raising funds for me since she was four years old. Today she is seven and has a wonderful personality that makes you feel youthful.

We all sometimes have to take a break from the old, mature mindset and act like a child. Having fun, being fearless, full of energy, and adventurous, and learning new things are all part of staying ageless.

Talking about feeling youthful, have you gone to your high school reunion? I went to a few, and the last one was my fiftieth reunion. Well, guess who was fun, fearless, adventurous, and ageless? Three girls that I graduated with had kept the youthful mindset as I had. Our personalities were so similar, and we had the best time! We became contagious in the group, making people laugh, sharing stories of good times, and keeping our bodies moving around like kids.

As I flashback to fifty-five years ago, I see that my mindset was determined to use my inner and outer beauty to overcome the harsh words that were spoken over me. Words that caused discouragement, insecurity, and failure were overcome just by focusing on the natural gifts God had given me.

There is a uniqueness in every one of us. God did not make us all the same. In the Bible it is said, “For You formed my inward parts; You covered me in my mother's womb. I will praise You, for I am fearfully and wonderfully made" (Psalm 139:13–14).

Fearfully when translated from the Hebrew refers to great reverence, heartfelt interest, and respect. *Wonderfully* when translated from the Hebrew has the meaning of being unique and set apart.

Every woman, child, teen, and man that has come through my doors at Safe Passage and my home has discovered the unique gift inside of them. I had the privilege to guide them in the positive godly way for which they were called.

Today, with over thirty years of experience in the non-profit world, I have helped people into new lives. Out of this came another project entitled "Time2Heal." Let me share how this came about.

On November 7, 2018, a mass shooting occurred in Thousand Oaks, California, at the Borderline Bar and Grill, a country-western bar frequented by college students. Thirteen people were killed, including the perpetrator, who died of a self-inflicted gunshot wound. It was a tragedy that caused the communities to mourn for months. I lived only twenty minutes away, and I came to support the families.

The next day, November 8, a fire started in Woolsey Canyon on the Santa Susana Field Laboratory property, a complex of industrial research and development belonging to Boeing, near the boundary between Los Angeles and Ventura Counties.

It was like a tsunami fire that burned 96,949 acres and 1,643 homes. Thousands of people were kept away from their homes for months. We took in our dear friends, Angelika and Eric, to stay with us during the burning blaze that hit Malibu Lake homes. During this time of the shooting and fires, I made myself available for prayer, reassuring people, and giving out goods for those in need. It took months and even into the following year for people to get back to their normal routines. Some did not have a home to go back to.

In January of 2019, at our monthly board of directors meeting, I shared with everyone my heavy burden for the people that had just gone through the trauma of loss. “We have seen so much tragedy in the past two months, and I want to be more effective in helping them heal. You all know that we have been successful for over twenty-one years in helping those who have been victims of domestic violence and abuse. Our program and counseling heal people’s past traumas. Now it is time for us to extend our services to those who have lost their loved ones and homes. This is trauma too.”

Within minutes, my husband, sitting there quietly at the board meeting, spoke three prophetic words: “It’s time to heal.” Sterling Williams, a board member and website designer, immediately looked up the phrase “Time to Heal,” and it was available to form a DBA. We took the phrase and turned it into a new project and website to serve the community with counseling to heal from past trauma.

My husband's prophetic words were directly from the throne of God. Here is what Jim was seeing in the spirit: "To everything there is a season, a time for every purpose under heaven: A time to be born, and a time to die; A time to plant, and a time to pluck what is planted; A time to kill, and *a time to heal*; A time to break down, and a time to build up; A time to weep, and a time to laugh; A time to mourn, and a time to dance" (Ecclesiastes 3:1–4).

These words resonated with everyone at the board meeting that night, and today Time2Heal is a trademark with its own website that has taken on the mission to personalize each person's journey, through counseling, mentorship, and empowerment, to the life they deserve. Thanks to beloved Sophie Turner, who spent endless hours and funds applying for the Time2Heal trademark. She is a legend and advocate for Safe Passage Heals! Her story will be told one day, as she is busy as a lawyer and mother of two and has a new man in her life.

I hope you are embracing this journey of my life story as an inspiration for you to be invincible. My journey continues today with new opportunities at age seventy. I can hardly believe it, that I have lived seven decades, with more decades that might still be enjoyed.

In the beginning of 2020, I was beginning to feel an urgency to get my vision board done, for it was on my New Year's list. I was invited to a vision-board class in Santa Monica, and it was an amazing experience. Have you ever done a vision board for yourself, for your personal goals for good health and inspiring surroundings of peace, love, and joy? I am not talking about goals to become wealthy, be an entrepreneur, get married, and travel around the world. I am talking about your soul, body, and spirit. If you are not whole inside, your life can never achieve happiness on the outside.

As I mentioned in the Introduction to this book, I was prompted to share my journey of inner healing and my mindsets of victory so that you, the reader, may be healed. Yet, I discovered that I had more healing to do as I sat in the class creating my vision board.

The attendees were all asked to paste our visions down on our boards, using photos related to health, environment, and physical endurance. Even though I was in good shape and healthy minded, there were still things that needed to be shifted around inside of me. For example, I needed to slow down and get balanced.

My vision board ended up being the highlight and inspiration of the class. I felt God using me to help those in the class who were stuck in their thinking. And again, this class turned out to be a new "Time2Heal" program, as we taught one other to put our vision boards together.

The following month, it was time for me to start looking for a new home to lease. I saw in my vision that I was to leave the city and move out toward Ventura County. By this time, COVID 19 was spreading across the world and into the United States. It was the most unusual time to be moving, with the lockdown quarantine. So many people were under fear and financially lost. Many were getting sick, and some were dying of COVID.

By the grace and mercy of God, I was able to move my family out of the big city and into the promised land of my vision. All because I stayed the course and did not allow my faith to be shaken.

"Assuredly, I say to you, whoever says to this mountain, 'Be removed and be cast into the sea,' and does not doubt in his heart, but believes that those things he says will be done, *he will have* whatever he says" (Mark 11:23).

There were many mountains I needed to speak to in order to get to my destination. Mountains of fear, catching COVID, keeping my business running, and not getting discouraged when being turned down, after looking for months for a new home.

Are you facing any mountains in your life? Do you believe that God is able to do the impossible? Do you have faith? "Now faith is the substance of things hoped for, the evidence of things not seen" (Hebrew 11:1).

On July 1, 2020, my family and I were able to make the exodus out of Los Angeles, the Egypt that symbolizes slavery to the world systems, and enter into a place of milk and honey, meaning richness of health and wealth.

Here I was starting the beginning of my retirement, with my daughters Michelle and Shawna and my beloved husband, who all stayed the course with me through the valleys and over the mountains. Our new neighborhood is amazingly peaceful and well kept, with each house looking perfect. The landlord was blessed to have us, for they were looking for a Christian family to rent their home.

The more I think about the move, the more I believe for a better life for my family and friends as we are still going through the COVID season. I had more time to pray and to organize my daughters' new transitions. Both daughters got new jobs and were able to meet like-minded people in our community.

My husband had his private office upstairs and conducted monthly Bible studies instead of weekly. I opened a new office in Thousand Oaks, just minutes away from our new home, and kept the office in the valley of Los Angeles.

As we watched and heard on the news of the COVID spread taking people's lives, my heart was moved to pray more. There were close friends getting sick, and some died—not of COVID but of other health issues. What has happened to our world? Where can we get some answers?

2020 was a year of chaos, division, fearfulness, isolation, hopelessness, and more! But for me, it was the opposite. It was a year of changes, rebuilding, relocating, praying more, and meeting new faces with the same mindset. That is one of the keys to a victorious mindset—to increase our faith with endurance and spending more time with God. Now, the time came, after being well established in my new home, office, and neighborhood, for God to shake up my daily routines. "I want you to write your life story based on the seven decades that you've lived. Share some history and your emotional issues that you have experienced in seventy years," God said to me. What? That would be too much work, and besides, I came out here for retirement. I left the busy city to get some rest and enjoy a life of leisure like most people in this area. God gave me more details, and I was getting more exhausted just thinking about it. This cannot be God, for He knows my plans to slow down and rebuild my home, family, and community.

Within a few days, His voice was clear to me and gave me the faith to pull through and write this book by October 1, 2021, just before my seventieth birthday. I was born on October 7 and turned seventy in 2021. The number seven symbolizes completion of creation—for me it meant not only completion of writing this book, but completion of a new, integrated vision of myself as a spokesperson, counselor, and specialist in my field of the non-profit world.

All the years of resources and life experience came together within six months, with the help of divine appointments, through new people and businesses that were inspired by my vision of the *Discover the Mind of Steele* book and website. God divinely appointed people, scenes, and productions to bring about this unexpected calling.

Now, it's your turn to take on *your* divine purpose and win the Crown of Glory: life. Here are some reminders to apply to your success:

Ageless: Think on these things: "*You are special.*" You are fearfully and wonderfully made. You can do all things through Christ. Keep your mind creating ways to improve yourself. Dancing, singing, exercising, and pampering your body keep you youthful. Age is just a number, and it's never too late to make changes.

Fearless: Have a childlike faith in trying the unknown. Push past your fears and say to the mountains: "Be removed!" Be the victor not the victim. There is a supernatural strength that comes from this. Set you mind on the finish line and see yourself winning!

Divinely Connected: Get connected with Jesus, for there is no other person on earth who walked in power, love, and miracles, sharing the example of a victorious life. Have a conversation with Jesus daily and include Him in everything you do. Once you create a relationship with Him, watch how He opens doors, gives you favor, heals your past trauma, restores your youth and years, and gives you the peace that we all seek after.

My conclusion: God chose me for such a time as this! How do I know this? He gave me the name Patricia: "noble one." I was born in October, during the autumn season, a month that was declared Domestic Violence Awareness Month in 1989. My favorite color is purple, which speaks of royalty, nobility, luxury, power, and wisdom. My calling (and yours!) according to Revelation 1:6 is to be a queen: Jesus "has made us kings [queens] and priests to His God and Father, to Him be glory and dominion forever and ever. Amen."

Discover the Mind of Christ Jesus

"FINALLY, BRETHREN, WHATEVER THINGS ARE TRUE, WHATEVER THINGS ARE NOBLE, WHATEVER THINGS ARE JUST, WHATEVER THINGS ARE PURE, WHATEVER THINGS ARE LOVELY, WHATEVER THINGS ARE OF GOOD REPORT, IF THERE IS ANY VIRTUE AND IF THERE IS ANYTHING PRAISEWORTHY—MEDITATE ON THESE THINGS. THE THINGS WHICH YOU LEARNED AND RECEIVED AND HEARD AND SAW IN ME, THESE DO, AND THE GOD OF PEACE WILL BE WITH YOU."

(PHILIPPIANS 4:8-9)

Trish Steele and Luisa Diaz, the founder of Mi Amor Gala, Celebration of Kindness.

About The Author

I am constantly astonished by the tsunami of energy that embodies Trish Steele. Her passion and purpose are driven by her need to help transform, uplift, and heal individuals who have experienced the harsh effects of trauma. As a pioneering force and a revolutionary voice, Trish carved out a powerful platform long before the advent of social media, including guest appearances, PSA's (Public Service Announcements) with major networks such as CBS and KCAL 9, radio, speaking engagements, and various forums, where she offered hope for those dealing with the stigma and pain of domestic violence, which she experienced in her own life. Her faith and perseverance to overcome insurmountable odds gave Trish the confidence to know that a successful, fulfilled life could be accomplished, no matter the circumstances.

Decades ago, Trish opened her home to mothers and their children seeking protection and care, while helping them establish bright, new lives for themselves. Safepassageheals.org, a nonprofit organization, was founded by Trish in the year 2000 to enable her to expand her ability to help as many people as possible. Her efforts have reached over two thousand individuals and families, with a 95 percent success rate. Her advocacy is far reaching, extending into other countries, such as Morocco. Trish has received many honors from various luminaries, government officials, and leaders. Of note are President Barack Obama, the Southern California Motion Picture Council, the Los Angeles City Council, the Trailblazer Award, the Beautiful People Awards, and the Life Member Order of Merit given by President Donald J. Trump, to name a few.

I'm proud and honored to have met such an amazing, shining, dynamic woman who has done so much to transcend the frailties of life, rectified with power, joy, and wellness. I am thankful for the amazing day that a client of mine in 2001 introduced us. My life has been more greatly infused and enriched with the beauty and power of service because of our many experiences working together to help make life better for those in need.

Trish, I salute your phenomenal seventy years on this planet, and I am proud to call you my friend.

Jeannie Jones, Image Advocate

Mr. and Mrs. Trish and Jim Steele make their grand entrance at Trish's
70th Royal Birthday Gala Celebration on October 7, 2021
Photo by William Kidstone

The Steele Family: Shawna, Trish, Jim, and Michelle at the Four Seasons Hotel, Westlake, 70th Royal Birthday Gala Celebration

Acknowledgments

God, thank You for creating me in a very special way to follow the mind of Christ! You gave me the courage and strength to write this book. You are God! Nothing is impossible for You.

Jim Steele, my husband, thank you for giving me your last name so I have the "Mind of Steele." Your wisdom and prophetic gifts have guided me to live in the perfect will of God.

My daughters, Shawna and Michelle, thank you for believing in me to write another book and to celebrate my biggest milestone birthday at seventy. Both of you will keep me young forever!

Amy Chinian, my dear friend and morning prayer partner, thank you for encouraging me daily to stay on the journey to our biggest desires in life. Thank you for being my friend for thirty-four years.

Angelika Holzaphel, my royal and loyal friend who descends from European lineage. We have big plans to get my message out to the unsaved world.

Jeannie Jones, my dearest friend, who saw so much more in me than I ever did. Thank you for enhancing the inner and outer beauty of my life, including this book. You are phenomenal.

Joanna Mastopietro, you are my rescuer in writing this book. Thank you for taking the time to edit my story in your late evenings and for turning my words into perfect descriptions of my heart's words.

Janet, Madalyn, and Kasey Cano, your support over the years with Safe Passage Heals has made a beautiful addition to my life and this book. Thank you for this.

Jan and Coco Wilson, thank you for the years of financial support when it was most needed. Jan, you are my son in the spirit and always will be.

Kathleen O'Donnell Dew, you came into my life at the perfect time when I needed divine help. You have given your genuine soul to our eternal friendship. Thank you for inspiring me to write this book.

Linda Dolson, you are the most amazing counselor Safe Passage will ever have. Thank you for being the best in your field for hundreds of women and children. I cherish our friendship always.

Luisa Diaz, my spiritual, loving daughter who always made me feel like a queen! Your encouragement while writing this book will keep me young forever.

Michele Jones, my Life Coach, who was divinely given to me by Kingdom Builders Academy. Your wisdom and coaching were a perfect fit for the title of this book.

My friends, who gave generously to support my seventieth birthday celebration and launch of this book!

Thank you for going above and beyond on October 7, 2021, to make this all possible in unusual times of COVID. Your faith and love will keep me going strong till the end. Your names are:

Luisa and Alan Brown

Janet and Kasey Cano

Theresa and Henry Robledo

Maria Primushko

Angelika and Eric Holzaphel

Christine and Ray Schwager

Theresa and Shihan Aluyen

Gail Nordskog

Stuart Craner

Bob Yerkes

Special thanks to **Joel Settles** for your gift in writing the Safe Passage grant applications and many hours spent toward the production of our events.

Cheryl Hiltzik of TriCuzz Productions, thanks for the many stories you put together on film to bring the best testimonies on the women at Safe Passage. You truly are a storyteller, the best!

The Zachariou Family (our friends from Greece), thank you for supported my vision for over twenty-seven years. And thank you for sharing your son Victor with me.

Vilma and Greta Zenelaj of Colored Films, your support and creativity for the Safe Passage women's testimonies have been amazing. Both of you are greatly appreciated.

Thank you also to **Michelle Shelfer** for the last-minute help in getting this book to press.

My board of directors of Safe Passage Heals.org, your time, love, funds, and support for over seven years—some over ten years—have kept me going with faith and commitment. I am blessed to still have you with me. Anna Stein, Janet Cano, Jim Steele, Michael Bernstein, Sterling Williams, Paul and Amy Chinian, Jeannie Jones, Theresa Gabriel, Martha Peretz, and Luisa Diaz.

Safe Passage / Women Crowned In Glory appreciates **Macy's**, **Obagi**, and **Jessica Simpson Collections** for seven-plus years of making abused women feel beautiful.

I would love to hear from you. Connect with me through social media or my website:

trish-steele.mykajabi.com/home

safepassageheals.org

time2heal.org

themindofsteele@gmail.com

Facebook: @TrishSteele

Instagram: @Trishjsteele

LinkedIn: @Trish Steele

To connect with Janet Cano:

Facebook: @JanetCano

Instagram: @JanetCano57

Trish Steele with Vice President of Safe Passage, Janet Cano, and her daughter Madalyn. You are seeing three generations of advocates against domestic abuse. Is it your Time2Heal?

Resources

National Domestic Violence Hotline

thehotline.org 800-799-SAFE (7233)

National Sexual Assault Hotline

800-656-HOPE (4673)

National Suicide Prevention Lifeline

800-273-Talk (8255)

Time2Heal.org

818-232-7476
Counseling and mentorship

Call for a free consultation.

Reverend Jim Steele for Spiritual Guidance

Truelifekingdom.org

Made in USA - Kendallville, IN
88675_9781801283359
09.02.2022 1542